ELECTRONIC
Music

Andy Mackay

ELECTRONIC

Music

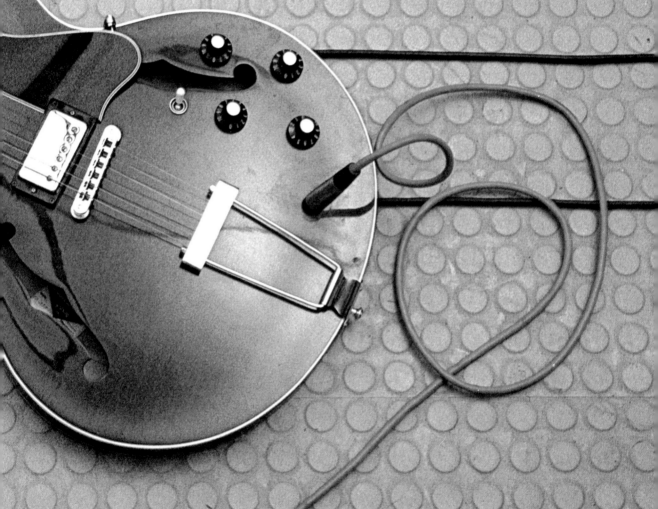

PHAIDON

First published in Great Britain in 1981 by Phaidon Press Limited,
Littlegate House, St Ebbe's Street, Oxford OX1 1SQ
ISBN: 0 7148 2176 4

Copyright © 1981 by Harrow House Editions Limited
7a Langley Street, Covent Garden, London WC2

General Editor Clive Unger-Hamilton
Art Director Nicholas Eddison
Designer Gillian Della Casa
Picture Editor Celia Dearing
Picture Researcher Lynda Poley
Research Assistant Jane Greening
Production Manager Kenneth Cowan
Production Editor Fred Gill
Editorial Assistant Sharon Bradley

Filmset by Facet Filmsetting, Southend-on-Sea, England
Illustrations originated by Hongkong Graphic Arts, Hong Kong
Printed and bound by Dai Nippon, Hong Kong

CONTENTS

FOREWORD

Most of the music we now hear is electronic, in the sense that the sound waves which strike our ears are generated by movements of loudspeakers from a succession of electric impulses. The technology of the recording studio and of broadcasting has a fascinating history which goes back to the last century. An understanding of these developments that have had such a profound effect on the performance and understanding of music is now as important as a knowledge of the instruments of the orchestra. This makes up part of the first section of *Electronic Music*.

But there are more obvious ways in which electronics have changed music. The invention of electronic performance instruments also goes back to the end of the nineteenth century: though some of the most ambitious projects are now forgotten, they were an inspiration to those who have developed the synthesizers that are so familiar today. Some of the instruments invented before the Second World War, in particular the electric guitar, form the basis of rock music: a new musical idiom and a new industry entirely dependent on electronics. The development of the tape recorder has led to the studio playing a crucial creative role in rock. I have set out to explain some of these processes, assuming no specialized knowledge of electronics (since I possess none myself). Wherever possible, I have also tried to explain something of performance techniques from a musician's point of view.

The availability of tape recording led after the war to revolutionary developments in the music of the avant-garde. The establishment of experimental studios and of electronics in performance has led to a great body of strange and exciting music (the full significance of which has yet to be felt). Live electronic music has used an astonishing range of new and modified technology in combination with brilliant visual concepts. Again these have been described as simply as possible.

Part Two of *Electronic Music* is a survey of the music that has been written for electronic resources. Composers have been faced with entirely new problems, both in performance and aesthetics. An understanding of these problems provides a key to music which often seems strange and disorganized.

Electronics has been closely linked with the most important movements in experimental music of the last few decades, particularly indeterminate music. Pop music, though its aesthetic has not been so vigorously polemicized, has nevertheless developed in ways which are more or less dependent on electronics. Film too has played an important part in developing new uses of musical technology.

The last part of the book consists of fifty biographies of important figures in the field, from inventors and composers to record producers and rock stars. The selection is by nature subjective, though I hope to have included the most important figures in the field of *Electronic Music*.

THE INSTRUMENTS

The extraordinarily rapid and imaginative developments within the field of electronic instruments were made possible in the first place by such revolutionary inventions as the phonograph and the telephone. In such a compact survey of the electronic musical technology of the present century, there is not room here for extensive coverage of scientists and inventors such as Alexander Graham Bell, Thomas Edison and Emile Berliner. This section treats first the remarkable history of electronic instruments, and then deals with the equipment of today's musicians, such as the commercial recording studio, the synthesizer and the increasingly fascinating applications of computers to music.

Thaddeus Cahill. His Telharmonium, the ancestor of Muzak, attracted nearly a thousand listeners to its first demonstration

THE HISTORY

The first electronic 'instrument' was the Singing Arc, the invention of William Duddell in 1899. Duddell was a young and distinguished physicist, commissioned to investigate an annoying side-effect of the new electric street lights. This was the tendency of electric arc lamps to emit an irritating whistle. As a by-product of his researches, Duddell built his Singing Arc as a scientific novelty, for use in lectures. He had discovered that the carbon arc lamp produced a note when a coil and capacitor were placed in parallel with it, the arc itself acting as a simple electrostatic speaker. By adding a keyboard to control the oscillations in the circuit, Duddell was able to play tunes on his remarkable invention (no illustrations of which appear to survive). The sound must have been somewhat unpleasant and incapable of tonal variation, for no musical or commercial development followed, though Duddell later increased the frequencies used to above the limit of human hearing, in experiments with 'wireless telegraphy' (as radio was known).

But Duddell's high-minded application of his discoveries to the service of pure science was not imitated by the extraordinary Thaddeus Cahill, who, in 1902, exhibited the prototype of his magnificent Telharmonium. This amazing creation, which its inventor called an 'electric music plant', was a synthesizer, weighing 200 tons, which was designed to be broadcast over the telephone; a working version of this behemoth was installed on Broadway by 1906, ushering in that mixture of artistic ambition, scientific genius and commercial sense that was to have the profoundest effect on all forms of music in the twentieth century.

The sounds in the Telharmonium were generated by inductor alternators, specific pitch being obtained from rotating cogged wheels that contained the same number of poles as the

After its initial success the **Telharmonium** had to be scrapped; it interfered with the normal telephone service

frequency required. (This system anticipated in several ways the principle of the familiar Hammond Organ.) The instrument was a true synthesizer – that is to say it provided a fundamental frequency, and multiples of that frequency as well as the means to mix them and obtain differing timbres of sound; but since electronic amplification was not then available, enormous amounts of power were needed. Each individual rotor (and there were enough of them, geared together, to produce all the notes through five octaves) was driven by a motor of 200 horsepower, and the resulting alternating currents were mixed in 4-foot-high iron core transformers. In performance, the Telharmonium used an organ keyboard but with thirty-six notes to the octave, making it extremely difficult for only one performer. Cahill believed that the only way to transmit music successfully was for the sound to be produced electronically at source; the only means then available was the telephone system. Accordingly, individual telephone-owners, as well as hotels and restaurants, were invited to subscribe; for a demonstration at the New York Electrical Society (and at other Telharmonium concerts), ordinary Bell telephone receivers were fitted with megaphones and concealed behind artistic arrangements of hydrangeas.

Audiences were overwhelmed by the purity of the sound, as well as by the mere fact of its transmission. The great virtuoso and composer Busoni, to whom Cahill gave a demonstration, was moved to write of it in his *Outline for a New Aesthetic of Music* (1907). Cahill's mighty invention eventually ceased operation, for it was interfering with the commercial telephone system. Even so, artistic limitations aside, it would have been made obsolete quite soon by the invention of the thermionic valve. This made possible the amplification of small currents, so electronic instruments of 200 tons could be reduced to a hefty but practical weight of a few hundred pounds. The Telharmonium was destined to be the only commercial non-valve (or non-transistor) instrument ever built.

In between the invention and the demise of the Singing Arc and the Telharmonium (and also, incidentally, of the magnetic recorder, which reappeared much later in a more potent and durable form, but which had first been patented in 1898 as the Telegraphone, see p. 23), various groups and individuals were extending the aesthetic boundaries of music, as well as rethinking the conventional use of traditional instruments in ways that, though not

Cahill's third, largest and final **Telharmonium** was this one, installed at Telharmonic Hall, New York, in 1906

themselves electronic, profoundly affected subsequent developments.

Looking back now, after three-quarters of a century, the vast and splendidly engineered bulk of the Telharmonium and its genteel rediffusion of what Cahill called 'high-class music' seems a characteristically Edwardian machine, reflecting the sturdy ideals of the nineteenth century. It was precisely these ideals that were being attacked in the years leading up to the First World War by visionaries whose fear was mingled with optimism for the future.

Orchestral music during the nineteenth century had shown an increasing concern with tone colour, both in new combinations of instruments and in a willingness to explore the possibilities of new instruments. (Berlioz, for example, began to use saxophones almost as soon as they became available.) By the end of the century, instrumental resources were as large and varied as could be imagined, and increasingly extensive use of percussion sometimes made even pitch secondary to noise, tone and rhythm. Richard Strauss's score for *Ein Heldenleben* (1898) provides a classic example: in addition to a huge string section, it calls for piccolo, three flutes, three oboes, cor anglais, two B♭ clarinets and an E♭ clarinet, three bassoons and a double-bassoon, eight horns, five trumpets, three trombones, two tubas, timpani, tenor drum, bass drum, side drum, cymbals and two harps.

Small wonder that some composers decided that music could move no further in such directions. It was this reaction, in combination with an increasing awareness of ethnic and exotic cultures, that led to a reappraisal of the uses of sound and structure in music. Debussy antici-

A Telharmonium rotor. Each rotor represented one fundamental note of the scale, and was geared, by doubling the number of teeth, to produce the higher octaves; eight octave levels can be discerned on the rotor above. The whole assembly was mounted on an 11-inch-diameter steel shaft over 60 feet long, and was driven by a 200 horsepower motor

(Top): **Alexander Scriabin** (1872–1915). He believed that his later music was the prelude to a supreme final ecstasy involving the whole of humanity. *(Below):* **Richard Strauss** (1864–1949). Although his music is deeply rooted in the traditions of Wagner, his scores often had some striking imitations of natural sounds, foreshadowing *musique concrète*

pated many later composers in his close association with poets and painters, while in the case of Scriabin, highly influenced by Debussy, it led to mystical and half-crazed ideas of a total synthesis of all the arts and senses. Tone colour became more important than ever before; such composers as Henry Cowell (1897–1965) began to experiment with 'tone clusters', groups of notes played on the piano by the fist or even the forearm. Not content with this, Cowell also explored the insides of the instrument, plucking and rubbing the strings. Most dramatic of all experiments with noise and natural sounds was the concert of factory sirens and steam whistles on 7 November, 1922, at Baku in the USSR. The factory sirens of the entire city were augmented by the foghorns of the Caspian Fleet, a battery of artillery, machine gunners and aircraft. These were conducted from the rooftops to produce a revolutionary celebration of socialist art.

Such approaches to musical thought, taking place at the same time as enormous advances in the fields of technology, made the eventual appearance of electronic music, in whatever form, almost inevitable. Early in the present

century, the most single-minded moves towards a whole new aesthetic of sound were made by the Italian Futurists. There was only one trained musician among them: Balilla Pratella, who wrote *The Technical Manifesto of Futurist Music* in 1911. It was in fact the painter Luigi Russolo who took the ideas of new music furthest with the manifesto *L'Arte dei Rumori* (*The Art of Noises*, 1913). His theories were backed up by the manufacture of 'noise boxes', discussed in his treatise, and with which he gave several concerts. The boxes were fitted with megaphone-like horns that amplified the various noise sources inside them, activated by handles. There was an Ululatore (Gurgler), a Sibilatore (Rustler) and a Scoppiatore (Exploder) among Russolo's numerous devices. Unfortunately, none of them is believed to exist today, though in 1914 their inventor gave a series of twelve concerts with them at the London Coliseum (now the home of the English National Opera). The two pieces performed, 'The Awakening of a Great City' and 'A Meeting of Motor Cars and Aeroplanes' have, in retrospect, the same feeling of false optimism that attaches to many of the Futurist

From a rooftop in **Baku**, the conductor directs a concerto for factory sirens and steam-whistles in 1922

14

Music of the Future, 1914.
Russolo's Noise Machines,
only days before war
broke out

paintings – of biplanes as the ultimate ideal of speed, or of guns as ultimate weapons. But future shock soon became nostalgia in the twentieth century. A few works in related idioms have proved more durable: Erik Satie's ballet 'Parade', for example, which incorporates a typewriter, revolver shots and a ship's siren into its seductive score. But shock they did and, more importantly, suggested the possibilities of music as an organization of all kinds of sound within the dimension of time.

But when, around 1920, the first commercial electronic instruments were manufactured, they were used much more by the classical establishment, and in Variety and popular music, than by the avant-garde. What is more, the immense scientific and technological break-throughs that had made them possible were the work of scientists and inventors, to most of whom the idea of electronic music as a means of entertainment had never occurred.

The behaviour of the sub-atomic particles called electrons has been at the heart of the most original and exciting scientific research of the last hundred years. Research into the nature of matter had led J. J. Thompson (Cavendish Professor of Physics at Cambridge) to the discovery, in 1897, of the electron. This was a minute, charged particle – smaller even than an atom – which in certain circumstances could flow or move at the speed of light, carrying with it a minute amount of energy. The existence of this electric energy in various forms had been known and studied since classical times; but the discovery that it could flow, and therefore transfer energy and information from one place to another, was crucial to the development of what we now call electronics. Further research into the nature of the atom and the behaviour of electrons led to both the theory of relativity and the quantum theory, and to a revolution in human existence without parallel.

In the early years of electronic research, scientists tended to work theoretically, inventors practically. (Until the Second World War, 'electronic' was a term used by physicists to describe the properties of the atom, rather than any devices using those properties.) Edison had discovered that electrons flowed between two terminals in a partial vacuum, in an opposite direction to the main current – the so-called 'Edison Effect'. Characteristically, he patented his discovery in 1886, though without understanding its cause, or having very much use for it. But it was this effect which led to Ambrose Fleming's invention of the thermionic valve, the first device in which free electrons were put to a practical purpose. This was a device to 'rectify' the current from radio waves: to allow it to flow in only one direction, hence the name 'valve'. The valve works on the basic principle that when a negative terminal (cathode) is heated in a vacuum, it discharges electrons through the vacuum to the positive terminal (anode). The flow can be varied by outside signals such as radio waves, and a switching effect could convert electrical impulses into such information as morse signals.

The decisive development in the field of thermionic valves came from the man whose name is most often associated with its invention, the American Lee De Forest. By adding a grid between the anode and the cathode in the vacuum tube, De Forest discovered that not only was the control of the current much more sensitive, but that the outcoming signals were amplified. It was this discovery which made possible electronic instruments, radio and all other fields of electronics, though it does not seem as if De Forest or anyone else realized the far-reaching implications at the time.

Transistors (which use semi-conductors for amplification) were invented in the 1940s and have largely replaced valves in most applications of electronics. The properties of certain substances to allow only a partial flow of electricity had long been known, and were used in crystal sets, familiar from the early days of broadcasting. They use a different principle to achieve the same function, which is the control and amplification of electrical impulses; but in spite of the efficiency and coolness of transistors, valves are still used in various applications – not least in the high-quality of the stage amplifiers used in rock music.

Technical difficulties, especially in obtaining vacuums, delayed the widespread manufacture of valves until the early 1920s, when they had reached a sufficient state of development to make possible the introduction of commercial broadcasting: in the USA in 1920, and by the BBC in 1922.

The next, and more important, wave of early electronic instruments was developed independently in several different countries between 1916 and 1930. The Theremin was invented in Russia by Leon Theremin and introduced in 1919; the Sphaerophon by Jörg Mager in Germany, who demonstrated it at Donaueschingen in 1926; Maurice Martenot presented the Ondes Martenot in France in 1928 (where a year later the pipeless organ of Givelet and Coupleux was also shown); Friedrich Trautwein had developed his Trautonium in Germany by 1930, the year after Laurens Hammond demonstrated in the United States the organ that bears his name (though it did not become commercially available there until

Lee De Forest with an early version of the triode valve. Originally designed as a superior form of detector, it was later found to be invaluable as an amplifier and oscillator, and as such was a fundamental item in early electronic instruments

Broadcasting in 1922. On the extreme left is W. T. Ditcham, who in 1919 was the first person to broadcast from Britain to America. Singing into the primitive microphone is the Danish tenor Lauritz Melchior, famous for his Wagner roles

(Above): **Leon Theremin**, inventor of the instrument which bears his name, and (top) a concert for two theremins with other musicians: Theremin, on the left, is performing and directing. (Left): A modern theremin, being played by **Youssef Yancy**

1935). Many modifications and some new instruments followed during the early thirties, frequently by the inventors already mentioned, though the Depression and later the approach of war slowed down and finally stopped development. The independence of the various inventors is shown in the wide variety of different methods devised for creating and controlling electronic sound. Such ingenious variety was not entirely the result of scientific enthusiasm: all of these instruments were made more or less commercially, and the securing of patents was an important consideration.

The Theremin, originally called the Etherophone, uses a relatively simple electronic principle to produce its sweeping and unearthly wail, familiar to aficionados of old science-fiction movies. It is unique in that the performer does not actually touch the instrument; there is a box from which an antenna, or aerial, projects, and the player changes the pitch by moving one hand closer to or farther from the antenna. The other hand controls the volume by its proximity to a metal loop. Such a mysterious and melodramatic mode of performance commended the Theremin to music-hall and Variety performers and even to Lenin, who impressed its inventor with his rapid grasp of its musical possibilities. Musicians intrigued by its new sound were further fascinated by the possibility it offered of infinite variations of pitch. The circuit inside consists of two oscillators tuned to a frequency well above the range of human hearing, one of which is fixed; the other, connected to the antenna, alters in frequency according to the proximity of any earthed object (normally the performer's hand). A difficulty in performance, later corrected, was a rather abrupt on-off switch, preventing any expressive attack or decay.

Friedrich Trautwein, with an impressive scientific background, did not have music as his principal concern in life. His Trautonium was a much more sophisticated device than the Theremin; using a neon tube (rather than a vacuum valve oscillator), the resulting wave form is saw-toothed and much richer in harmonics. Different timbres were obtained by making the harmonically complex sound progressively more simple by the use of filters and other devices. This process is known as subtrac-

The background music to **The Day The Earth Stood Still** includes four theremins and a sine-wave generator

18

Friedrich Trautwein, professor of acoustics at Cologne University and inventor of the Trautonium, here supervises one of his students at the instrument. *(Below):* A view of the console of a trautonium made by Telefunken in 1933. The instrument could produce a surprisingly wide range of timbres

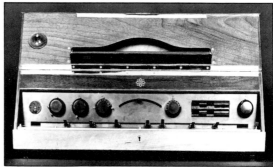

tive synthesis. The instrument was fairly difficult to play with any degree of competence, but it was quickly accepted by the German musical establishment. Pitch was controlled through a ribbon device operated by the right hand; higher harmonics were added by the left hand operating a series of studs. Hindemith wrote a Concertino for Trautonium and strings (1931), and Richard Strauss incorporated it into his Japanese Festival Music (1940). Its versatility helped it last well into the 1950s, being utilized in the new, purely electronic studio music, particularly in the improved form of the Mixtur-Trautonium, developed by Oskar Sala.

Jörg Mager, more than Theremin, saw electronic instruments as extending the range of facilities available to serious composers, particularly in the creation of microtonal intervals, and his instruments were made principally for such high-minded purposes. Both the Sphaerophon and a later instrument, the Kaleidophon, are played from a keyboard, though glissandi are available – and in the case of the latter, glissando chords. Their sound generation is by the use of feedback generators. Mager was commissioned to produce the bell sounds in a Bayreuth production of *Parsifal*.

The place held in Germany by the

(Right): Jörg Mager's **Kurbelsphaerophon** of 1923 was one of the first electronic instruments. Its sound was restricted, however, to a single melodic line. *(Below):* A later invention, the **Partiturophon,** was capable of playing harmonies and was used to perform keyboard music

Sphaerophon and the Trautonium was filled in France by the Ondes Martenot. Maurice Martenot's intention seems to have been to create an instrument which, though as dramatically exotic and new as possible, could nevertheless be related to traditional performance and manufacture. Its shape was both elegant and sensuous. Its sound transducer (resembling an art-deco lyre) is in fact an acoustic resonator with sympathetic strings to enhance the sound and give the instrument its characteristic timbre. The principle resembles the use of two high-frequency oscillators in the Theremin, which in this case are controlled from a seven-octave keyboard. There is also a ribbon-like device, running the length of the keyboard and played with a kind of thimble, which made available such effects as a vibrato or a glissando. Himself trained at the Paris Conservatoire, Martenot was particularly concerned that his invention should be accepted as an instrument meriting the serious attention of musicians and requiring a comparable academic training given to other more conventional instruments. To this end he prepared a teaching manual for the instrument (which boasted an introduction by the great pianist Alfred Cortot) and founded a school of instruction: L'École d'Art Martenot. His efforts were rewarded when many leading French composers wrote for the Ondes: Milhaud, Honegger, Ibert and, most notably, Messiaen. The organ of Givelet and Coupleux, on the other hand, was principally interesting for its use of punched paper rolls, controlling four oscillators; a method which anticipated the control systems used in early synthesizers (and in more recent computer systems). One was installed in a Paris broadcasting station and another in a local church there.

The Hammond organ was much more of a commercial enterprise than any of the instruments described above. Its phenomenal success was due to brilliant engineering and care in manufacture, rather than to any totally new ideas (although this is true to some extent of all the early instruments, whose makers were applying such principles as valve oscillation rather than inventing totally new concepts). The sound in the Hammond organ was produced by rotating cogged wheels passing a magnet, creating alternating currents at a particular frequency – principles very similar to those applied by Cahill in his Telharmonium. By providing the player with the means of mixing the fundamental tone with various harmonics, by use of 'drawbars', a wide variety of tone

(Above): **Mlle Ginette Martenot** playing the instrument invented by her brother in Honegger's *Joan of Arc at the Stake,* and *(right)* the cartoonist Hoffnung's impression of the instrument. *(Below):* An early electronic organ found an unlikely enthusiast in **Goebbels,** when he investigated it in 1936

(Above:) **Bruno Helberger** and the Hellertion. It was played by pressing a fretted leather band; it could play chords

(Below): **Carl Bechstein**, the grandson of the founder of the Bechstein company, and the **Neo-Bechstein piano**. This instrument has no soundboard, but has a traditional piano action; the vibrating strings are amplified electrically, as with the electric guitar

was available to the skilled performer. The characteristic vibrato sound of the Hammond organ is largely due to its use in conjunction with the ingenious Leslie loudspeaker cabinet (see p. 40). The problems involved in making a versatile, polyphonic keyboard instrument which remained reliably in tune and was reasonably easy to operate were quite formidable; it is a tribute to the ingenuity and skill with which Laurens Hammond solved them that (in spite of many new modifications) Hammond organs essentially the same as his original 1935 version are still widely used.

'While the Hammond organ is played like a pipe organ, it is not made in imitation of it,' proclaimed the Hammond Instrument Company when first marketing their new product. But in fact the majority of the early instruments were installed in sacred rather than in secular surroundings; it was not for another twenty-five years, when such musicians as Jimmy Smith and Karlheinz Stockhausen exploited its possibilities (in very different ways) that the potential of the Hammond as a new voice was realized. The instrument proved more durable than its many rivals produced in the years after 1935. Their sound was produced in a variety of ways: electromagnetically activated reeds (Wurlitzer, Everett), frequency division of oscillator-generated frequencies (Baldwin, Vierling), rotating electrostatic generators (Compton) and various photo-electric systems, as in the Welte and the Rangertone. Electronic technology was also used to produce improved versions of familiar instruments. Most successful of these was the 'Neo-Bechstein' piano, which although shaped like a grand piano had no metal frame or sounding board, using instead magnetic microphones placed above the strings to pick up the sound, which was then amplified. Wooden hammers were used, giving great dynamic control. It was rapturously received by many musicians. Development of electronic keyboard instruments continued up to the early 1950s, notably with the Melochord of Harald Bode, but also with various instruments aimed at a more popular audience.

In the period leading up to the Second World War, some composers and performers had accepted and used the electronic instruments made available to them. But alongside, more readily apparent developments were taking place in films and radio, which in technique and approach anticipated many of the post-war resources. Film, particularly, had opened up a whole new field of exciting possibilities, and there were men of vision to exploit it.

The fact that film passes through the projector at a regular number of frames per second had suggested to various observers that, since different pitches and timbres are generated by more or less regular oscillations of the air, if the regular visual images could be converted to sound, music could be created by drawing patterns directly on to the film. (The principal technical requirement for this, a light-sensitive cell which converted pulses of light into pulses of electricity, had been invented – in a relatively inefficient form – as early as 1905.)

László Moholy-Nagy, a prominent artist and designer connected with the Bauhaus movement, had suggested the possibility of the graphic production of sound in 1922. His theatre works combined reflecting images and amplified music; but his efforts in combining sound and film took a rather indeterminate approach to the music, using such images as profiles and fingerprints as the source material. More successful innovations were being made in Russia, where film as a medium was taken more seriously than elsewhere. In Leningrad in 1930, the musical theorist and mathematician Avraamov was demonstrating 'Ornamental Animation in Sound', using geometric figures to create music. Pitch was controlled by the distance of the image from the camera, and volume by the exposure. The most sophisticated of several other Russian experiments was Voinov's bank of eighty-seven drawings graded in semitones, used to interpret such pieces as Rachmaninov's C♯ minor prelude.

In Germany, Rudolf Pfenninger independently developed a similar system, with drawings used as a basis for creating either sine or saw-tooth waveforms. This method was used in a film of the early 1930s, 'Tonende Handschrift', featuring Handel's *Largo*.

The first man to draw sound directly on to film was the Australian Jack Ellit, working in London in 1933. But in America, James and John Whitney developed a highly original method of creating, from animated film, the regular patterns needed for the generation of musical notes. This involved the use of a pen-

(Above): **Guglielmo Marconi.**
(Right): The **Marconi-Stille tape recorder**, used by the BBC. (Below): An early 'professional' tape recorder

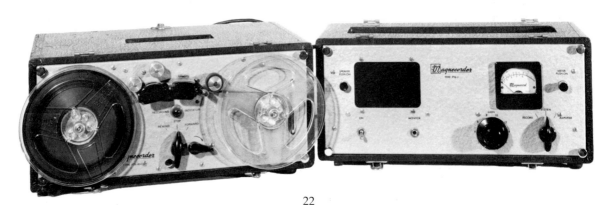

dulum device: the swing of a pendulum, explained John Whitney, was in essence the same as the 'swing' of the string on a violin or a guitar – except that it was very much slower. By recording such a movement on the film soundtrack and speeding it up about sixty times, the varying (but regular) patterns of light and dark could be turned into sonic frequencies. The Whitneys used this method to create the soundtrack along with the required sounds. But John Whitney has devoted many years to the technical and aesthetic problems of directly relating aural and visual images: he has created new sounds by graphic methods, and has made visual interpretations of existing music using more advanced technical resources, including computers.

Another important animator who has concentrated on the creation of sound directly from film is the Canadian Norman McLaren. His technique uses a library of cards, each displaying graphically a sound waveform; used in this way, film can become almost a musical instrument – until the synthesizer, this was the most practical way of creating new sounds.

Gramophone records, though manufactured electrically after 1924, were still reproduced entirely mechanically, though with great ingenuity in the construction of the devices. This included the application of the electrical theory of matched impedances to the construction of tone arms and speakers only one year after the introduction of the first electrical recordings; partly to cope with the greatly increased bass response and overall volume, which caused earlier models to jump. The (by now) highly profitable industry was only too pleased to market new machines.

The only application of the gramophone in the creation of serious modern music (passing over Respighi's use of a recorded nightingale in *The Pines of Rome*, 1924) was experimental work with variable-speed turntables, by such composers as Milhaud and Hindemith in the 1920s. More importantly this technique was used (together with RCA test tones and other sounds) by John Cage in his *Imaginary Landscape No. 1* (1939). But these were merely the imaginative and rather desperate efforts of frustrated men, who had to wait until the availability of the tape recorder and the development of the first electronic studios in the 1950s before their aural imaginings could be made concrete. Overall, the gramophone contributed little or nothing to the development of the new music.

During the 1930s there were many important inventions and developments which, although they were later to have a great impact on music, did not have their potential fully realized until after the war. These included the electric guitar, the electronic piano and electric amplifiers; television, experiments with stereo and, most important of all, great advances in magnetic tape recording.

In the early 1940s, intelligence officers monitoring German radio broadcasts were puzzled by the continuity and quality of sound in transmissions which, although they realized could not be 'live', nevertheless lacked the surface noise and discontinuity to be expected from gramophone records. The puzzle was solved when in September 1944 the Allies captured Radio Luxembourg (which had been under German control) and found magnetic tape recorders far more advanced than any in use before the war. Meanwhile, in England, members of Coastal Command were listening to another great technological advance, which had been accelerated (like many other advances in the electronics field) by the war effort; the first 'full frequency range' disc recordings of the sounds of British and German submarines. These training records had been commissioned from Decca by the RAF, who needed a new degree of fidelity in order to make the very subtle distinctions in sound between the combatant submersibles. The German Magnetophones were cumbersome, noisy and needed banks of amplifiers, and the Decca records were still at 78 rpm; but new standards had been set which offered the recording industry a challenge it could not refuse. The response to this challenge after the war led to a revolution in both popular and art music.

Neither development was entirely new; indeed the most important of them, the tape recorder, pre-dated almost every other invention in electronics and music. An American, Oberlin Smith, made the earliest discoveries with 'magnetographic sound recording' in 1888, and his discoveries were soon followed by the patenting of a practical machine by Danish inventor Valdemar Poulsen. This device, the Telegraphone, was exhibited at the Paris Exhibition of 1900, where it was awarded a Grand Prix. Although Smith had suggested the use of cotton impregnated with steel dust as the material for carrying magnetic impulses (a suggestion which anticipated the modern use of magnetic oxide), Poulsen used steel wire. Ordinary carbon telephone transmitters were used to convert sounds into electrical impulses, and a Bell telephone receiver was used to convert the impulses back into sound, which, incidentally, was the essential weakness of the Poulsen system since it could not cope with a frequency range sufficient to reproduce music with any degree of fidelity. This made it in effect a dictating machine, and it was used as such in various forms until the 1920s, when its use was generally discontinued. The totally mechanical phonographs of the day still reproduced music more convincingly, though had the valve amplifier been available to Poulsen, the development of music reproduction and of electronic music might have been quite different. As it was, research and production of magnetic recording machines slowed down almost to a standstill until the early 1930s.

The discovery in 1927 that the addition of a frequency above the limit of human hearing, the bias tone, greatly reduced noise on recordings, suggested further possibilities for the use of magnetic tape with music. Research was also carried out into the use of magnetic sound in films, notably by Kurt Stille. This method, which still used steel wire, was not a great success; the use of magnetic sound in films did not become widespread until the early fifties. However, Stille sold the rights to his work to the Marconi Company, who in 1934 produced the Marconi-Stille steel tape machines, used by the BBC for many years. These machines had many disadvantages – not least the fact that since the tape ran at sixty inches per second, a reel of tape with thirty minutes' running time weighed thirty-five pounds.

Other research carried out at this time resulted in the ingenious Philips-Miller system in about 1936. This used a chisel device to cut patterns into plastic tape which were read using a light-sensitive scanner, rather like a film sound track. It was with this equipment that the first stereo recordings were produced.

More significant in the long term was the development in Germany of magnetic tape coating, patented in 1929 by Fritz Pfleumer. Initially paper tape was used, but soon afterwards this was replaced by plastic in the first modern tapes. It was this development that led to the production of the Magnetophone as a dictating machine in 1935, and the debut of a far more advanced model some six years later.

All modern tape recorders, whether a pocket cassette or multi-track studio machine, work on the same basic principles. The tape is made of an acetate base, evenly coated with a magnetic oxide; it can then be magnetized, just like iron or cobalt. The tape is moved at a constant speed past magnetic heads, with the assistance of various devices to keep it at a constant speed and tension (hence the complicated threading). The first head which the tape passes is the erase-head – a plain magnet which can remove previous recordings; next it passes the recording head – this converts electric impulses from a microphone or other source into magnetic impulses, which are recorded on the tape in sequence as it moves steadily past. The third head is the playback head, which picks up the magnetic impulses and reconverts them to electrical impulses. These can then be amplified and fed through a loudspeaker, reproducing the original sound. Tape can be stored almost indefinitely, unless it becomes exposed to a magnetic field. This, incidentally, can include

The piano has long been notorious for being one of the most difficult instruments to record successfully; it has a wide tonal range, complex harmonics, and the sound is produced over a relatively large area. This technician, recording directly on to the wax cylinder of an Edison phonograph, has an unwieldy answer to the problem

flying over either of the Earth's magnetic poles.

The modern tape recorder was born in the broadcasting studio, and was quickly accepted by the major broadcasting concerns. Radio shows in the USA were taped from 1947 (using the newly developed 'Scotch' brand of tape), though for some years after this the BBC were continuing to work with the fearsome Marconi-Stille machine, which used steel razor tape running at a very high speed. This was rightly considered such a threat to human life, should it break, that it was operated from a separate room. There was spot-welding equipment on hand in case of this not infrequent occurrence.

The record industry initially saw tape as a dangerous rival, and it was partly this fear that speeded up the introduction of microgroove records. Yet within a very few years of the launching of the first LPs in 1948, it had become an important part of the making of records. Discs no longer had to be directly recorded on to a master, but could be recorded first on tape; it was this new control and freedom that made the tape recorder one of the principal tools with which, over the next two decades, a new popular music was created. However, in an industry controlled by large corporations, changes were very slow.

The composers of the serious avant-garde needed far less time to realize that this was the instrument of their dreams. The first composition entirely for tape was realized in 1948, by Pierre Schaeffer; and the composer who had been waiting longest, Edgard Varèse, began in 1950 on a work to involve tape. By the early 1950s, the tape recorder had spawned two very different types of studio.

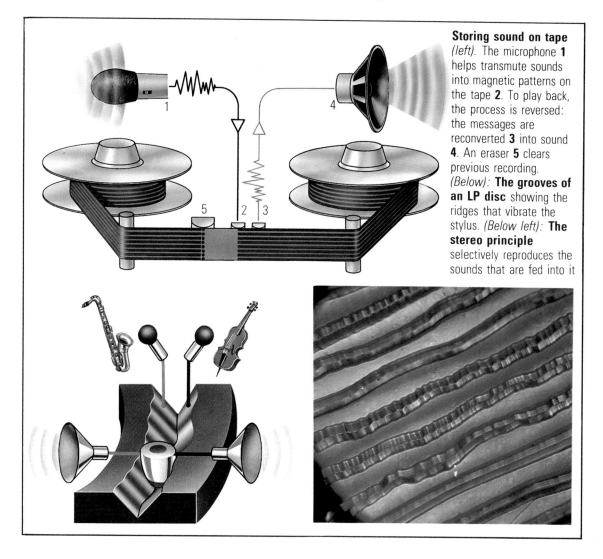

Storing sound on tape (left). The microphone **1** helps transmute sounds into magnetic patterns on the tape **2**. To play back, the process is reversed: the messages are reconverted **3** into sound **4**. An eraser **5** clears previous recording. (Below): **The grooves of an LP disc** showing the ridges that vibrate the stylus. (Below left): **The stereo principle** selectively reproduces the sounds that are fed into it

The recording studio has two essential parts, a soundproof chamber fitted with microphones, and the control room housing the recording and playback equipment. To get the best possible sound, each instrument is recorded separately on to its own narrow strip of the master tape. The saxophone player, isolated acoustically, listens through headphones to the keyboards, which are fed directly into the mixer without using microphones (direct injection). Key: **1** soloist; **2** keyboard player; **3** engineer; **4** mixing desk; **5** 24-track recorder; **6** loudspeakers; **7** soundproof window

THE COMMERCIAL STUDIO

Even after the introduction of tape recorders into the commercial studio in the late 1940s, the process of recording remained much the same as it had been in the years before the war. It was still a continuous process, the aim being to get the best possible performance in one 'take', since the disc from which all records would subsequently be made was cut at exactly the same time as the music was being per-

formed. Any mistake meant that the piece had to be begun again (or, as was very common, the recording was issued preserving the mistakes for posterity). Recording had been electric since 1924, meaning that the microphones were sent through a valve console, which basically controlled the volume. By the early 1950s this method of recording had achieved a very considerable degree of fidelity, while tape recorders and even electrically driven disc-cutting lathes were still considered somewhat unreliable. At EMI's

amous Abbey Road Studios, records were still cut directly on to wax discs on a lathe driven by a weight descending from the ceiling. (The discs were kept warmed for use at 100° Fahrenheit in a thermostatically controlled cupboard.) Moving-coil mikes going into a four-channel desk were used, but since these mikes picked up sound from all directions, the use of more than one often confused the sound rather than clarified it.

It was the introduction of stereo which indirectly gave record producers the possibility of using the studio in a new way. The principle of stereo is based on the fact that in a concert hall, or indeed in any room, sound bounces backwards and forwards off the walls, striking the ears from all directions – in the same way that light would be reflected in a mirrored room. By turning our heads we are able to locate the main source of a sound, but the overall effect is created by the complex pattern of reflections; the long reverberation of cathedral music dying away in some lofty Gothic recess, or the punch of a rock band in a cellar.

Early stereo consisted of two simultaneous recordings taken from different sides of the room, which, when played back from separate speakers, partly re-created the feeling of space and depth. The two tracks were, to all intents and purposes, separate

Two electronic instruments which can be directly injected are the synthesizer *(above)* and the Lyricon *(right)*, an electronic wind instrument. Rock guitarists, however, usually prefer to hear the sound they get through an amplifier, causing headaches for the recording engineer especially when the sound is modified by the use of special effects such as fuzz, wah-wah, reverb or tremolo. These are often operated from a pedal console *(left)*

recordings; there was no chance of mixing or modifying them during or after performance.

From the recording point of view, the introduction of stereo did not create any fundamental changes. Microphones had to be positioned with even greater care, and the purely technical aspects of recording had to be given close attention. But with the increasing preoccupation with 'hi-fi', particularly among buyers of classical records, meticulous attention to such aspects of recording was fast becoming a prerequisite.

What gave a fundamental change to recording technique was the possibility that, since pop records were still issued in mono (as they were until the early seventies), the two tracks available for stereo could be used to make two separate recordings at different times, which could be mixed together later. In practice, this usually meant one track for instruments and another for vocals. This may not seem revolutionary, but for a group like The Beatles – who both played

instruments and sang—it was a big advantage.
George Martin, The Beatles' producer, used the
technique as soon as it was available to him. (There
were unfortunate consequences when, some years
later, the records were issued in 'stereo', with all the
instruments on one side and all the vocals on the
other.)

In America, stereo produced recording facilities
with an extra track. This was the three-track recording, on half-inch tape, which was used from around
the mid-fifties until the introduction of four-track in
the early 1960s. The thinking behind this demon-
strates the relatively greater importance given to
popular music in the United States. In Britain, as
already mentioned, the main use for stereo was
always seen to be symphonic and operatic recording
(apart from records for railway fetishists of the Flying
Scotsman steaming through their living-rooms at
record speed). But the USA, with such bankable

be combined and balanced through the mixer before
recording on to standard quarter-inch tape. The engineer
selects the mixer's mode *(above)* before balancing and
equalizing the tracks *(below left)*

artists as Sinatra and Nat 'King' Cole, found that
stereo spread between vocals and orchestra led to
problems in featuring the voice. The answer was to
create an extra track 'in the middle' for the singer
backed by an orchestra in lush stereo.

This gave an even greater freedom to American
pop producers than that offered by two-track, and
one that was exploited in brilliant fashion by the first
great creative producer in rock, Phil Spector. He
always worked in mono and, from around 1963, while
in his early twenties, produced a string of hits for The
Crystals and The Ronettes which established once
and for all the potential of the recording studio as a
creative tool in its own right. These records, 'Be My
Baby' or 'Da Doo Ron Ron', had a sound totally unlike
any possible live performance; huge amounts of
echo, reverb and careful mixing blended voices,
guitars, strings and other instruments into a 'wall of
sound' in which the individual characteristics of the

The engineer, producer and an anxious musician listen to a
playback through a pair of ordinary domestic loudspeakers,
the kind that the majority of record buyers are likely to
possess. Selected tracks of the 24-track tape *(below)* will

instruments were largely lost. Against this were unsophisticated but powerful vocals, and the whole was backed up by thunderous drums.

Whereas whole albums were commonly made in a morning, Spector needed days to make a single. Since the technique of overdubbing several sounds on the same tape could not be much used (due to a build-up of tape noise), large numbers of musicians were needed: two drummers, several percussion players, two pianists, backing singers, sax players, etc. On the earlier records, which were recorded on three-track, two tracks were used for the instrumental backing – which was then 'bounced' down to one track. Another track was then used for the vocals, after which both tracks were mixed down on to the third track, adding more echo or other effects. An important device much used during this period was the limiter. This is an electronic device which 'squeezes' the sound, preventing the loud peaks from being too *forte*, and thus allowing the overall volume to be greater. Some equalization was also available; it was originally necessary to compensate for the tendency of tapes to record and play back some frequency bands more efficiently than others. The playback was equalized (EQ'd) to reproduce the original sound. Now it is widely used to alter sounds, highlighting or pulling back any desired instrument.

But in general, tone control and effects had to come mainly from the positioning of the microphones. These techniques are still very important today, often giving the 'trademark' of a particular engineer or producer, even though a great many more devices are available than there were in the mid-sixties.

The next generation of studios, coming in around 1963, used four-track recording on inch-wide tape. This was important for the sound quality, especially when there was overdubbing. Although overdubbing (or double-tracking) had been used since the 1950s, it revealed a fundamental weakness of tape recording. This was the so-called 'signal-to-noise' ratio: when a tape is recorded, a certain amount of noise is generated by the interaction of the recording head with the tape. As each successive track is recorded, a hiss builds up. Unfortunately it does so in the ratio of the square of the number of tracks; one overdub, and the noise is twice as bad; four, and it is sixteen times worse. The greater the width of tape available, the better will be the quality of the recording. For this reason, with four-track recording using inch-wide tape, several overdubs could be achieved. This technique was taken very close to its limits in recording The Beatles' *Sergeant Pepper* album, completed over many months in 1967. The technique was, in simple terms, to record on all four tracks and transfer them to one or two tracks of another four-track machine. This left spare tracks available which could be used

The engineer can add another dimension to the recording at the mixing stage by giving it 'presence'. This might be done electronically, or as shown opposite, by playing the recording into an echo chamber, where the sound is reflected round the room and recorded again

and transferred (with the original mix-down) to another machine. The four composite tracks would then be mixed to stereo. All this was very time-consuming, especially since the *Sergeant Pepper* album used a lot of special tape effects as well as orchestral and other instruments. Its effect on record-making was enormous; studio and tape techniques became a standard part of rock music.

The Beatles were not the only innovative group at this time. In the previous year, Brian Wilson had spent an unprecedented six months recording The Beach Boys' monumental hit single, 'Good Vibrations', which featured a Moog-theremin and a cello in its complex texture. However, eight-track was available even before *Sergeant Pepper* was finished, and as extravagant multi-tracking became *de rigueur* it was soon followed by sixteen-track.

Since 2-inch tape was (and still is) the widest which manufacturers found practical, there was an inherent problem: that the noise of all sixteen tracks became concentrated in the final stereo mix. This was solved by the introduction of the Dolby noise reduction system, which, by a rather complicated process, effectively cut out noise. This facilitated the move to twenty-four track, which remains the current standard (although more tracks can be obtained).

If considerable emphasis seems to have been given to the studio and to the use of multi-tracking, this is because it is the key to developments in rock since the mid-sixties. Like a sculptor modelling in clay, the musician is now able to build – upon the armature of a rhythm track – a full three-dimensional structure. Quadrophonic sound, which was the sensation of the early seventies, was laid to rest a few years later – the little-lamented victim of bickering between rival manufacturers.

Of the range of sophisticated devices used in studios to treat and modify sounds, only a few need description. Echo and reverb are the old warhorses of rock records, described by one studio musician as 'the opium of the producer'.

Phasing, the distinctive 'whooshing' effect often heard (particularly on drums) in the psychedelic era, can be produced in the traditional way, using two tape recorders very slightly out of synchronization with each other, or it can be produced digitally.

In fact many of the most original and effective sounds on records come from experiment or accident, such as an instrument accidentally overheard in a corridor.

THE CLASSIC STUDIO

The first music which owed both its generation and its aesthetic entirely to electronic equipment was created in France in the late 1940s. Pierre Schaeffer, a sound engineer with the French broadcasting service, Radiodiffusion-Télévision Française, presented a 'concert of noises' using sound-effects records of natural sounds in 1948. (There was an echo here of the Futurist noise concerts over thirty years before, which Schaeffer readily acknowledged.) The following year experiments with organizing pre-recorded 'everyday' sounds continued at the radio station, using tape recorders; this led to the creation of the first electronic studio. The term *musique concrète* was coined, to indicate that the music was being actually created on tape without origins in musical notation or any abstraction. (The term later came to be used to distinguish music using a montage of sounds from music made using purely electronically created sound.)

The basic studio equipment consisted of several tape recorders with variable speeds, microphones and other recording facilities, tape editing equipment and devices for mixing and playing more than one tape at the same time, so that cross-fades and superimposition could be carried out.

With these relatively simple resources, astounding transformations could be wrought on the original sounds, which Schaeffer often obtained deliberately from mundane and familiar objects. These were carefully catalogued by Schaeffer, whose combination of whimsy and pedantry is seen in the *Étude aux Casseroles*, which uses saucepan lids as its main sound source. The techniques used for modifying sounds included speeding up and slowing down the tape, altering the pitch, reversing the tape and playing the sounds backwards, the addition of echo and reverb, and, of course, strange juxtapositions and superimpositions. Schaeffer worked closely with the composer Pierre Henry soon after the studio was established, and in the succeeding years many of the leading composers of the European avant-garde worked there.

In Germany a different approach to tape composition was being formulated. This was to involve the use of sounds that were generated purely electronically. Germany enjoyed a tradition of serious scientific interest in music and electronics, and also in the establishment of educational institutions for research and experiment in the arts. Work at the Bauhaus, and in the experimental radio department at the Musikhochschule in Berlin in particular, had a great effect on electronic developments.

One of the key figures in Germany after the Second World War was Werner Meyer-Eppler, a distinguished physicist and Director of the Institute of Phonetics at Bonn University. Following a demonstration in 1948 of the Vocoder, an analytical device which included an artificial voice, Meyer-Eppler became increasingly interested in the musical possibilities inherent in the synthesis of sounds. He published a book, *Electronic Tone Generation, Electronic Music and Synthetic Speech* the following year, and in 1952 collaborated with Bruno Maderna in what became known as the first piece of electronic music in Europe, Maderna's *Musica su due Dimensione*. A year later the first studio for the production of purely electronic music was set up in Cologne. It was at this studio, shortly afterwards, that Stockhausen and others began working on some of the classic pieces of electronic composition. Cologne remained the centre, for the next few years, for the creation of pure electronic music using strict serial methods of composition, while for many years Paris remained the home of *musique concrète*.

Since, in the Cologne Studio, sound was being created electronically, in addition to recording equipment such as was found at the Paris RTF studio there were various tone generators and other devices for modifying sound. But in order to understand the aims and the techniques of the composers of pure electronic music in the early 1950s, it is necessary to explain some principles of sound synthesis.

ACOUSTICS AND SYNTHESIS

When an instrument plays a note, its pitch is determined by the frequency of regular vibrations of the air that are created: sound waves. The more frequent the vibrations, the higher the note. Sound waves are in fact cycles of alterations in air pressure: compression followed by rarefaction. Amplitude (loudness) depends on the amount of energy in each movement. The human ear can perceive sounds from about sixteen cycles per second (a very low note) up to about 20,000 cycles per second (an extremely high-pitched note). The upper limit in particular varies considerably from person to person, and declines quite sharply with age. The term Hertz (Hz) is used to describe the number of cycles per second; middle C for example is 264 cps or 264 Hz, and the A above it (which is used everywhere as a tuning standard) is 440 Hz.

But along with the frequency of the main note are various other frequencies sounding simultaneously, though they are quieter and not generally perceived as separate. The basic frequency is called the fundamental, and the other (higher) frequencies are known as harmonics or overtones. These harmonics occur as specific multiples of the basic frequency: if the basic frequency is A 440, the harmonics will be 880 (the A one octave above), 1320 (the E above that), 1760 (the A above that and two octaves above the fundamental) and so on. As the harmonics get higher they get closer together, but also relatively quieter. The sequence of these intervals is known as the harmonic series. The mathematical ratios which govern the harmonic series had been studied since the time of Pythagoras, but it was not until 1701 that it was fully formulated by French scientist Joseph Saveur. It was realized that although all the constituents of the harmonic series up to the limit of hearing could be theoretically present, they varied considerably in their relative strength; it was these variations that were responsible for the characteristic sound, or timbre, of an instrument. The design and construction of instruments reinforces particular frequencies; whether they are made of wood or of metal, the shape of the bell or the mouthpiece, even the type of varnish on a violin will cause the instrument to resonate more strongly at some frequencies than others.

The fewer harmonics present, the purer a note sounds, approximating to the timbre of a flute or a soprano voice. Alone throughout the whole of music, the electronic oscillator can produce a note totally devoid of harmonics: the sine tone. It soon became apparent that by using sine tones and combinations of harmonics in varying strengths, the so-called formant spectrum of an instrument could be approximately re-created. This principle, known as additive synthesis, was used by Cahill in his Telharmonium and by Hammond in the Hammond Organ. In a reverse situation, some harmonics can be removed from a harmonically rich sound by the use of filters: subtractive synthesis. The composers of the Cologne Studio were able to take the principle further

and create entirely new, artificial sounds.

But the principle of producing a note synthetically is more complicated than simply the arranging of a harmonic structure. The characteristic timbre of an instrument is also affected by the relative loudness of its component frequencies over the period of time in which it is sounding; this is known as the envelope of the sound. Most instrumental sounds start quickly, and die away over a longer period; this build-up to the maximum volume is known as the attack, after which the note may remain steady for a while before starting to decay. Different frequencies within a sound may decay at different rates. The envelope varies considerably from one instrument to another; for example a guitar has a rapid attack and begins to decay almost at once, while a bowed violin has a slower attack, a slightly longer held time and a quicker decay.

In addition the sounds of most instruments also contain noise, particularly in the attack. Noise, acoustically speaking, consists of irregular vibrations of the air, as opposed to the regular vibrations which produce musical pitches. Untuned percussion instruments (the side drum or cymbals, for example) produce sounds consisting almost entirely of noise, usually with a very short attack time. To further complicate the final sound which reaches the listener, notes played together have a mutual effect on each other, called modulation. It is this modulation that gives a group of violins a different sound from a single instrument. Even this very basic description of acoustic phenomena gives an indication of the complex and laborious tasks facing the composers of the Cologne Studio in the 1950s.

The first director of the Studio, Herbert Eimert, reinforced his very influential theories with a concept of 'total serialism' as a basis for construction of electronic works. The composers of the Second Viennese School, led by Schoenberg, had evolved, in the early years of the century, a method of composition which used all twelve notes of the scale in a series, or tone row. (The later works of Webern were particularly influential on the early electronic composers.) This method involved various quasi-mathematical structures such as inversion or reversal of the notes of the tone row. The post-war serialists such as Boulez and Stockhausen used serialism in their piano pieces, extending it to a sequence of relative volumes, and sometimes textures as well. The precision achieved by the electronic studio now made possible further pursuit of total serialism.

Most of the basic electronic tone generators in use at this time had been designed not for the production of music but as laboratory test equipment. Although cumbersome in use for the purposes for which they had *not* been intended, their high technical standard and accurate calibration made them well suited to the demands of the scientifically minded young musicians of the early 1950s. Though there were electronic instruments of an earlier era available, such as the Trautonium, these were quickly abandoned in favour of the sine wave and pulse generators. The basic equipment in the earliest period consisted of the above-mentioned generators, a white noise source and various filters, as well as several mono tape recorders and later a four-track recorder.

Later in the decade, electronic music studios were established in many European countries. The most significant were those at Milan (1955), Philips at Eindhoven in Holland (1955–60 and thereafter at Utrecht), and in Sweden. In the USA several private studios were in existence by the early 1950s, including the one used by John Cage and his colleagues, and that of Edgard Varèse, both in New York. There was also the commercial studio of Louis and Bebe Barron, where the music for the film *The Forbidden Planet* was created.

Two of the major pioneers of tape music in the USA, Otto Luening and Vladimir Ussachevsky, frequently shifted their (very basic) recording studio from one private house to another in their car, and ended up in the basement of the conductor Toscanini's house in New York. It consisted principally of one Ampex 400 tape recorder, and with it they produced the tapes for a concert at the Museum of Modern Art in October 1952: the first public concert of tape music in the United States. Their music was produced from conventional instruments such as flute, voices and piano – simply but effectively transformed into new sounds by tape manipulations and a few devices, including a kind of reverb box. The Barrons used electronic generators as the sole sound source of their music, and were the first people in America to do so. Cage, from his earliest tape pieces ('Imaginary Landscape no. 5', 1952, and 'Williams Mix', 1953–54) used natural sounds, instrumental sounds, noises, electronic sounds and extracts from previous compositions: virtually the whole range of available audible material. These were juxtaposed and mixed, with a great deal of tape splicing (according to chance operations).

The European distinction between *musique concrète* and pure electronic music, therefore, never developed in America. In any case, by about 1956 it was no longer very relevant in Europe, though it probably continued to affect styles of electronic composition in Paris or Cologne for a while longer. Technically the most advanced studio in Europe during the late 1950s was the RAI (Radio Audizione Italiane) studio in Milan, founded by Berio and Maderna in 1955. Although both these composers had worked mainly at Cologne, the Milan studio favoured no particular approach to composition. Cage himself was one of many composers to work there later in the decade.

But though there was no prejudice in the sound sources of American electronic music, there was a wide divergence of compositional methods, ranging from strict serialism to complete indeterminacy. The divergence was heightened in the next stage of development as universities became the main sponsors of studio facilities, and as the technology became increasingly sophisticated.

After several years of working in living-rooms, Luening and Ussachevsky found a home for their rapidly expanding studio facilities on the campus of Columbia University. Academic interest in electronic music was particularly strong at Toronto (where Hugh Le Caine worked, creating new instruments as well as music on tape) and at the University of Illinois. Pioneer work was being done there with computers, under the direction of Lejaren Hiller and Leonard Isaacson; their efforts were paralleled in some respects by the work of composer and mathematician Milton Babbitt at Princeton, who had been interested in electronic music since the 1930s.

In 1955 RCA demonstrated a synthesizer which had been developed by Harry Olsen and Herbert Belar. Knowing that Babbitt was interested in working with it, Luening and Ussachevsky suggested the formation of a joint university council for electronic music, using as part of its resources the RCA synthesizer. The Columbia-Princeton Electronic Music Center was set up in January 1959, and soon became the most important centre for electronic music in the United States.

Since then, the use of synthesizers has become synonymous, to many people, with electronic music. It is essential to understand what synthesizers are, to comprehend how they have become both the Ariel and the Caliban of modern music-making.

The oscillograph or soundwave pattern produced by a synthesizer imitating a saxophone *(above)* has a general outline resembling the peaks and troughs of the more complex contours produced by the true saxophone sound *(below)*

AMPLIFIERS AND LOUDSPEAKERS

The only way in which electronic and electro-acoustic instruments can be heard is through a loudspeaker, whether from an instrument, tape or disc. Amplifiers are the lungs of electric instruments, speakers their vocal cords and larynx. A great deal of costly attention has understandably been paid to their development, especially by the manufacturers of the main commercial instruments and in the rock studio, as well as by hi-fi manufacturers.

The history of the electric speaker goes back, remotely, to Bell and the invention of the telephone in the 1870s. The moving-coil speaker was patented in 1898, although the combination of amplifier and speaker for general use dates from 1929, the year in which mains-operated radios were marketed. Sounds had been amplified for thousands of years (starting with cupped hands) by use of an expanding horn or funnel, and ending considerably after the start of the electronic era with the sophisticated horns of the gramophones of the 1930s. This included the remarkable Stentorphone or Antexophone, which by the use of an air compressor amplified sounds to a public-address level. A Stentorphone was installed at Bexhill, England, in 1913 which could be heard two miles away. The principle of the electric loudspeaker owes little to the horn principle, except in powerful speakers for very low frequencies, which, because of the long wavelengths involved, need a certain length; and in some speakers for high frequencies, which are very directional.

Although a relatively simple, even crude, electro-acoustic device, the basic design of the speaker has not changed for more than fifty years. A loudspeaker is a transducer: a device which converts one form of energy into another. In this particular transducer, the energy is in the form of electric impulses which are transformed into sound waves. The process by which the impulses arrive at the loudspeaker involves a whole chain of transducers. For example, the movement of a violin player's arm, a pianist's hands or a sax player's lungs is transferred via a string or reed into vibrations of the air. A microphone converts these vibrations into electric impulses, corresponding to the frequency of the notes involved. After their strength has been increased by an amplifier, these impulses are again converted by a loudspeaker into movements of the air to be picked up by our ears and converted into impulses of the auditory nerves which the brain finally interprets as a violin sonata or a sax solo.

In a loudspeaker, a cone of some flexible material (usually cardboard or paper, but occasionally plastic or metal) is suspended in a rigid frame. Behind the centre of the cone is a coil of fine wire; any backward or forward movement of this coil will produce a corresponding movement of the cone. Behind and around the cone is a permanent magnet. When a current passes through the coil it becomes magnetized, positive or negative according to the alternations in the current. If the current produces a polarity opposite to that of the permanent magnet, the coil is attracted; if the polarity is the same, it is repelled. The electric current thus produces a physical movement, which the flexible cone transmits to the air as sound waves.

The amplifier was one of the first composite

Unlike the classical guitar, the electric guitar has no soundboard, and without electrical amplification the sound produced is almost inaudible

The feeble vibrations are picked up by electromagnets. The tone and quality of an electric guitar largely rests on the precision of its pick-ups

The impulses are fed into an amplifier. It is at this stage that the tone might be modified by adding fuzz, wah-wah, reverberation and vibrato effects.

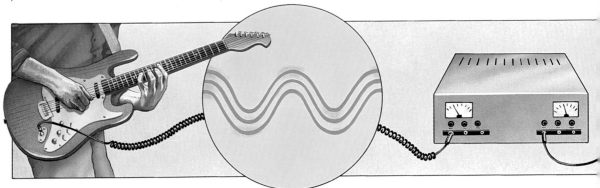

An amplifier from the early days of broadcasting, used to step up the weak signals received from the aerial

Early **wireless receiving equipment** needed cumbersome accumulators, which had to be charged frequently

electronic inventions. The discovery that signals coming out of a valve could be stronger than those going in was put to use almost immediately it was known. The first valve amplifier had been made by De Forest in 1912, although practical models only became available in the 1920s, with the start of commercial radio broadcasting. Even these earliest amps were capable of amplifying a minute radio signal to audible level, which represented an immense increase.

The design and structure of amplifiers and loudspeakers has a great effect on the way they perform. The frequency range of early speakers was not very large; nor did it have to be, since recording and broadcasting equipment was relatively inefficient. The human ear is able to hear sounds ranging from approximately 20 cycles per second to about 20,000. The full range of frequencies which could be recorded in the thirties (whether acoustic or electric) was about 30 cps to 8000 cps, and acoustic speakers could often only handle 100 cps to 5000 cps.

The guitar, being a middle-range instrument, did not require a particularly large frequency range and presented no great problem to early manufacturers who, needing effective amplifiers and speakers as an essential adjunct to their new instrument, created some of the first specialized speakers. The famous guitar manufacturer Leo Fender started making amplifiers in 1948. These had built-in speakers in the same cabinet, as did most amps of the period. Guitar

The resulting amplified current, perhaps mixed with the impulses from other instruments, is now directed into the loudspeaker

The variation in current causes a metal core attached to the loudspeaker diaphragm to move to and fro

The vibrating diaphragm sets the air in motion, which in turn eventually reaches the eardrum; the brain interprets these vibrations as sound

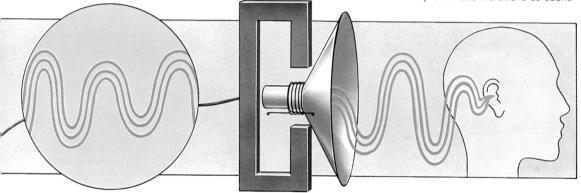

speakers have increasingly aimed for high volume, and for a certain amount of distortion to produce the sustained sound guitarists want.

Another application of speaker technology to a specific purpose was the ingenious 'Leslie' cabinet, nearly always used in conjunction with the Hammond organ. Because listeners were accustomed to hearing pipe organs in large, reverberant buildings (with a resultingly complex pattern of echoes), the sound of electric organs coming out of inadequate speakers in smaller rooms was flat and unimpressive. This was solved in the Leslie by mounting two speakers on a rotating bearing. As the speakers go round and round, the sound is modulated, i.e. a subtle interaction of pitch and volume is set up. Variations in pitch come from the Doppler effect, the rapid movement having the same effect upon the ear as a speeding police car. Variations in volume too are caused by the simple mechanical movement; the sound is, as it were, thrown back on itself, creating a rich, chorus-like effect. Some modern speakers (like one manufactured by Yamaha) create similar effects entirely electronically, by shifting the sound rapidly from side to side between two fixed speakers.

A close-up of the highly sensitive **electromagnetic pick-up**. The Neo-Bechstein piano operates on the same principle

Booming its disembodied voice from the clouds, this RAF Victoria, fitted with amplifiers and loudspeakers, was found to be an effective means of controlling rioting tribes in the remoter areas of Afghanistan

THE ELECTRIC GUITAR

Rock music, of course, developed in performance as well as in the recording studio. It is broadly contemporary with avant-garde electronic music, and just as much a product of the new technology. Electric keyboards, echo and reverb units, and the surprisingly versatile combination of microphone and amplifier all played a part; but the dominating instrumental voice was that of the most exciting new instrument of the century, the electric guitar.

The inventors of the electric guitar in the 1920s and early 1930s would not have connected the sounds of rock and roll with their 'frying pan' and Hawaiian guitars (sometimes made of aluminium or Bakelite, incidentally). However, Leo Fender and Les Paul, whose names are associated with the development of the most successful modern guitars in the early fifties, must, like Dr Frankenstein, have had some conception of their conception's ultimate power.

The reason for the guitar's success is that, although it gives a purely electronic output, the signal is created in a most human way. It is therefore suitable for almost any electronic treatment while remaining capable of expressing the individuality of the player. It is also relatively easy to play, but able as well to demonstrate the highest virtuosity. Sexy, noisy

The electric guitar. The body-shape **1** is traditional, but the inward curve enables the hand to reach the strings more easily. There is no soundboard, and instead the bodywork concentrates on stability. The fingerboard **2** is strengthened by a steel bar. The strings **3** are attached to worm-gears, known as machine heads. Electromagnetic pick-ups **4**; the placing of the pick-up affects the tone. This guitar has a combined bridge and tailpiece **5**. The strings pass over the individually adjustable saddles *(a)* and are secured by nuts *(b)*. Socket, jack and lead **6** connecting the guitar to the amplifier. Pickguard **7** to protect the body and cut out electrostatic interference. Volume and tone controls **8**, and pick-up selector switches

and modern, it inevitably became a symbol of youthful rebellion; but unlike the saxophone of the previous century, it was never treated with condescension for not being a member of the symphony orchestra.

Unlike the acoustic guitar, from which it inherits its general design, the electric guitar has no need of a large sound-box to amplify the sound produced by the strings. Instead it has electromagnetic pick-ups under the strings near the bridge. The most common type of pick-up consists of a magnet wound round with copper wire. The vibrations of the strings induce a current in the assembly which is transferred to an amplifier and thence to a speaker.

One of the most important characteristics of the electric guitar is its ability to sustain a note. This is a form of feedback, reinforced by the solid body of the instrument (generally made of a hard, heavy wood such as mahogany).

Pick-ups and guitars were developed by many different people from the 1930s on. Although Fender and Paul are the most familiar names, much credit is due to De Armond, who invented an efficient pick-up in 1931; Fred Tavares, who designed probably the most popular of all electric guitars – the Stratocaster – in 1954; and Seth Lover and Ted

McCarty, who invented the 'humbucking' pick-up in 1956. The latter is a very powerful pick-up with less hum and more sustain and distortion, making it very popular with rock guitarists – particularly as amplification became more powerful during the late 1960s.

The electric bass guitar developed slightly later, and is still occasionally known by its original name of Fender bass. It was not accepted in rock music as readily as the guitar, possibly because bass speakers were relatively less efficient in the 1950s, and old-fashioned (upright) string basses were still used for some years. But the electric bass's superiority on stage and in the studio soon became apparent. Its structure and electronics are essentially the same as the guitar, though like the orchestral double-bass it has only four strings. In the studio it is very often 'direct injected' into the console, without the use of an amplifier, giving a purer sound which can be modified at will.

THE SYNTHESIZER

Although the Telharmonium, the organ of Givelet and Coupleux and various later devices have been described as synthesizers, in that they create particular tones or timbres from the most basic sources, the modern use of the word is much more specific. It refers to an electronic device which contains in one unit, or series of linked units, all the resources necessary to generate and modify sounds electronically. A synthesizer is in effect a complete electronic studio, although without the recording facilities. Given the complexity and untidiness of the early studios, their development in some form was inevitable, even though the earliest examples were far from compact – often filling, if not a whole room, at least an entire wall.

However, even the earliest electronic synthesizer (the RCA Mk 1 machine developed by

Olsen and Belar in the early 1950s) had considerable advantages over existing studios. The various elements of the synthesizer were compatible with each other, and could be used to act upon or in conjunction with other elements within the device; and, more importantly, the synthesizer could be precisely programmed in advance by the composer. In the RCA machine this was done by the use of punched paper rolls (used much earlier in the Givelet and Coupleux organ), which, although laborious, appealed to the composers of strict serial music who had access to it, since it gave precise values to every aspect of a composition: pitch, volume, duration and timbre. Milton Babbitt was the most notable composer to take advantage of this.

The RCA Mk 2, which was installed at the Columbia-Princeton studio in 1959, had a more sophisticated programming system, using a binary number system on punched cards. As well as tone and noise generators, it possessed the ability to process outside sound sources through microphone inputs. Although quite complicated to programme, it was capable of high-quality synthesis of some familiar instrumental sounds as well as being admirably suited to the realization of total serialist pieces. It was, however, superseded in flexibility and ease of operation by the next synthesizers, which used the principle of voltage control.

Robert Moog, whose name has become as synonymous with synthesizers as that of Biro with the ball-point pen, published a paper entitled *Voltage Controlled electronic music modules* in 1964, and constructed a voltage-controlled oscillator the same year. (A few years before, German engineer Harald Bode, who constructed equipment at the Cologne studio, had suggested much the same process.) The construction of voltage-controlled instruments was soon taking place in a number of countries. Voltage control was not a new principle, though it had not been applied to electronic instruments. Before it was used, electronic sound-generating devices had to be changed and set manually, by turning a dial or flicking a switch. By using a change in voltage to produce the same effect, the operation is carried out not only very much faster but with greater accuracy as well. The way in which a voltage can convey such information can be understood if the flow

Perhaps the best known of all electronic compositions is the theme tune for the BBC TV series *Dr Who*. It was produced at the BBC's Radiophonic Workshop using an early form of synthesizer similar to the one shown above

of electricity is seen as pressure, analogous to the flow of water in a pipe. As the pressure is increased or decreased, or the direction of flow is changed, the device upon which it acts responds with a corresponding change in its performance. An obvious example is a keyboard connected to an oscillator; as the keys operate changes in voltage in prearranged steps, so the oscillator produces frequencies corresponding to different pitches. The process is something like the way in which a dimmer (rheostat) on a light switch produces different intensities of light as it is turned. Control voltages can also act as a 'gate voltage', starting and holding a function for as long as required; or as a 'trigger voltage', switching a function on or off with successive impulses. Synthesizers can also convert an audio signal into an active control voltage by means of a frequency follower (which converts pitch to voltage) or an envelope follower (which performs the

Peter Zinovieff has been one of the most imaginative pioneers in the field of electronic music in England. His Synthi 100 *(above)* was one of the first to analyse and synthesize sounds

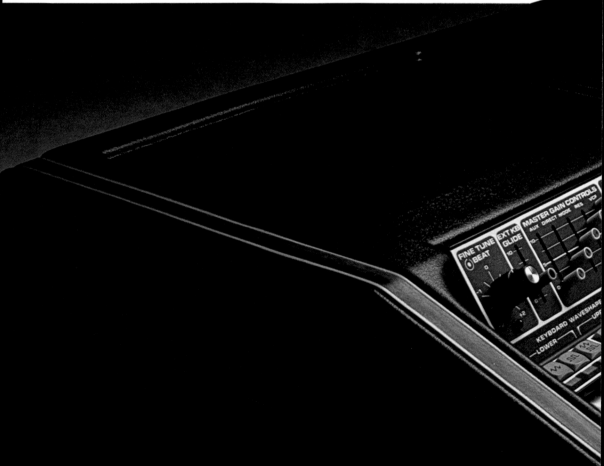

same function of conversion for volume).

The really interesting aspect of voltage control becomes apparent when one considers that since every component produces a voltage, it can therefore act upon any number of other components. This is where the modular concept (used in all synthesizers after Moog's first models in 1964–65) has such an advantage.

Paralleling the set-up of early electronic studios, all synthesizers contain four basic types of component: signal generators, devices to modify signals, devices to control signals, and mixers. (They also contain amplifiers, and sometimes their own speakers as well.) These components are arranged as modules, a series of relatively simple circuits which can be inter-

connected to produce complex effects. This means that by adding other units, a range of synthesizers of increasing complexity can be readily created.

An example of one of the most basic and widely used techniques involving the use of one component to control another is the use of one oscillator to vary the frequency of another. This is called frequency modulation. The output of an oscillator is the voltage equivalent of its waveform; if this is slow and of quite low amplitude (volume), and is applied as a control voltage to a 'signal oscillator', the result will be the small, regular variations in pitch heard as vibrato. Because in order to produce vibrato the frequency of the oscillator must be slow – too

The solo performance synthesizer aims at producing a melodic line with as wide a tonal variety as possible. The player can select with ease the type of attack and decay, the number and type of harmonics, and also whether the overall tonal shape changes or remains steady

The ERA light-show performers
giving a spectacular display of laser
effects to accompany 24-hour racing
at Le Mans. An acousto-optical system
translates sound waves from recorded
music (usually filtered to avoid a
garbled result) into light pulses; these
are bounced off vibrating mirrors to
produce a kaleidoscope of
sound-wave patterns

slow to produce an audible note – synthesizers have special sub-audio generators included for this (and also for many other control functions). These may go down to a frequency of only one oscillation every five seconds.

When frequency modulation is applied with oscillations within the audio spectrum (about 20 cps upward) then the signal oscillator is not merely changed in pitch, with the timbre remaining the same; new 'sideband' frequencies are produced that change the tone, and result (if the control frequency is increased still further) in distorted, bell-like sounds. These sounds, which have been very widely used in electronic music, are further exploited in another circuit amost invariably found in synthesizers: the ring modulator. In this, the original frequencies of two inputs are entirely lost and replaced with new frequencies resulting from the interaction of the original notes and their harmonics (the

sum and difference tones). Again the sound is rich and bell-like.

Voltage control of amplification results in the articulation of a synthesizer. This is largely achieved by the use of envelope generators, which control the attack and decay of a sound, although this can be done in very complex ways. Variations in tone or timbre are achieved by using a range of different waveforms going through a wide variety of filters, as well as by modulation. Unlike the case of the classic studio, where complex waveforms that make up instrumental or vocal sounds were produced from a large number of sine wave generators (by building up the harmonic series), synthesizer manufacturers use oscillators producing more complex waveforms and alter them by filtering. The basic sounds used are a square wave (with a sound rather like a clarinet), a sawtooth wave (with a buzzing sound) and also sine waves, though these are used mostly as control oscillators.

Given that all of these effects could be operated simultaneously, and that they could interact upon each other simultaneously, the potential of the synthesizer to produce new and intriguing sounds was very soon apparent. But the airy unpredictability of experiment soon gave way to dull and unimaginative repetition. At the same time as Herbert Deutsch was working with the first Moog, Morton Subotnick with the Buchla and Babbitt with the RCA, two of the first available Moogs had been sold to producers of TV jingles. The modular concept of the voltage-control synthesizer made it ideally suited to commercial development; and by the early 1970s a very wide range of 'performance synthesizers', having a limited number of pre-set programmes, was available. The ARP, the Roland and the Oberheim, as well as the Mini-Moog, were all widely used; each had a slightly different sound, and each had its protagonists, in much the same way as pianists continue to argue the relative merits of a Steinway or a Bechstein. The English manufacturers EMS produced cheap and portable machines which were still relatively unpredictable in programming, including developments of the quaintly named Putney (and its accompanying keyboard, the Cricklewood). EMS also developed one of the first synthesizers to include a computer, the Synthi 100, designed for and used in 'serious' electronic studios.

All synthesizers up until the early 1970s were monophonic: that is, they could only play one note at a time, albeit a complex one. This meant

that records such as Walter Carlos's *Switched on Bach*, which played a great part in making the sound of synthesizers overfamiliar, had to be made by overdubbing each instrumental line separately in the recording studio. The earlier performance synthesizers were in effect simple versions of studio machines, and as such were limited to the relatively narrow range of sounds which have become associated with their use, particularly in popular music.

The availability of sophisticated polyphonic machines, such as Sequential Circuit's 'Prophet', which can be pre-programmed with a very wide range of sounds, from principally a solo instrument (not unlike the use of the Theremin as a novelty earlier in the century) to that of an ensemble instrument. In this capacity it is almost as familiar as the guitar in popular music, the ghostly sound of the 'string synthesizer' being particularly hard to avoid. The enthusiasm with which film composers had used nearly every means of electronic music production almost as soon as it was available, increased still further with the possibilities offered by these obedient machines and their ready supply of sonic thrills.

Since there is no reason why a control voltage may not be set in motion by means other than a keyboard or a dial, various types of synthesizer have been specially developed for other instrumental performers. These include 'syndrums', used with uncanny predictability on dozens of Disco records. In these, which resemble in appearance a small set of tom-toms, the impact of the drummer's stick on a rubber or plastic pad closes a circuit which triggers a pre-set sound. Probably less widely used are guitar synthesizers, some of which have ribbon controls on a simulated guitar neck, while others treat sounds created by a normal guitar. The Lyricon is an ingenious wind synthesizer designed to be played like a clarinet. Breath and lip pressure are converted into voltages which control loudness, attack and vibrato.

The use of a pitch-to-voltage converter will allow any instrument to act as a trigger for any synthesizer set-up. But, like most of the instruments described above, this has its greatest appeal for rock musicians. Composers and performers in the avant-garde who found packaged electronics too constricting developed a different aproach to live performance.

In this light show display given by ERA, the sound source is a live performance given by Tim Blake in his *Crystal Machine* concert

LIVE ELECTRONICS

For the first fifty years all electronic music was, of necessity, 'live'. Until the end of the 1950s, most composers used electronic instruments in the same way they would have used conventional instruments, although exploiting the new range of timbres, pitch and power that they offered. There were notable exceptions to this in America, where nearly all innovations in the use of electronics in performance have been made, many of them by members of the 'school' which centred around John Cage. Cage initiated a new field of music when in his *Imaginary Landscape No. 2*, written in 1942 (a series begun in 1939 using among other things variable-speed gramophone turntables), he specified the use of an amplified coil of wire, and in the *Imaginary Landscape No. 3* the use of a contact mike on a marimbula. The traditional balance of instruments could now be completely altered. Minute, almost inaudible sounds could be enormously amplified, sounds never before thought of as musical could be used. In fact the entire audible world with which we are constantly surrounded became available to the composer. The results in performance were sometimes unpredictable, a fact welcomed by Cage, though not by many other composers at the time.

Technically a large part of the development of avant-garde electronic performance has consisted of the application of existing technology to new methods of use. This has often been in direct contrast to the high technology of commercial instruments. Even after the availability of synthesizers and other specially made pieces of equipment, composers and performers have continued to modify existing devices, or manufacture their own out of existing elements. The strong iconoclastic element, and a professed admiration of amateurism in Cage's musical philosophy, encouraged such radically new uses of existing equipment and the production of customized devices.

Cage's *Cartridge Music* (1960) used gramophone cartridges to amplify sound sources enormously. An earlier work, the *Imaginary Landscape No. 4* (1951), uses radios. This score specifies twelve radios with twenty-four operators, controlling volume and tuning independently. (Delays in starting the first performance meant that most of the radio stations had stopped transmitting, resulting in a particularly sparse landscape.)

Before electronic
technology became readily
available, **John Cage**
strove to achieve new
effects by mechanical
means

(Far right): Four portable
radios play a central role in
a performance of
Kurzwellen (Short Waves)
by **Stockhausen** *(below)*

Although Cage's role in the development of new musical technology has been partly inspirational and theoretical, his close involvement with other artists (by no means all musicians) has resulted in the creation of many specially designed circuits. Of the musicians associated with him, the pianist and composer David Tudor has been outstandingly innovative in his use of new equipment (and also in new ways of playing old equipment). Although described as a pianist, Tudor is the most widely experienced and skilled performer in avant-garde music, using a bewildering range of electronic devices and performance set-ups, both with Cage and in his own and other people's compositions, many of which have been specially written for and dedicated to him.

Another pioneer of live electronic music who worked in America was the extraordinary Australian pianist and collector of English folk songs, Percy Grainger. In 1935 he wrote *Free Music,* using four theremins, and in 1948 constructed, with Burnett Cross, a Free Music machine, using oscillators.

For most avant-garde composers, it was not until they turned with enthusiasm a few years later to the long-awaited tape recorder (with the possibilities for control that editing and mixing gave), that the most innovative aspects of electronic music began to be realized. For a while electronic music, particularly in Europe, was confined to the studio. Within a few years, however, even in Cologne, where pure electronic music was being produced with puritanical fervour, the need was felt for some element of live performance. This was the result partly of artistic and partly of practical considerations.

Although many studios were owned by broadcasting networks, the amount of air-time available for such uncompromising music was nevertheless quite limited. Similarly, record companies were not overenthusiastic about issuing recordings with no potential sales. It began to be realized therefore that although works were being created directly on to tape, there would still sometimes be a need to play them to an audience in a concert. Loudspeakers made a poor, even ludicrous, substitute for musicians, and it was realized that either tapes needed the augmentation of performers, or that works originally composed on tape should be presented in a 'performance version'. One of the first of all pieces to use electronically prepared tape, Varèse's *Déserts,* was based on the contrast between an ensemble of conventional instruments, and music from a loudspeaker.

The use of instruments with prerecorded tape became extended to include the use of tape machines to record and play back during performance (as in Kagel's *Transicion* in 1959). Live electronic music developed also in Japan, where in 1961 Takehisa Kosugi wrote a piece – *Micro I* – for solo microphone. Toshi Ichiyanagi, a pupil of Cage, wrote several pieces for electronically modified moments, both Western and Japanese, starting with *Space* in 1966. Of works transcribed from pure studio electronics to performance of tape with live performers, Stockhausen's *Kontakte* (1959–60) was one of the earliest.

Stockhausen's live electronic music developed from his studio experience. *Kontakte* did not involve any sounds being electronically produced actually during performance; *Mikrophonie I* (1964) was Stockhausen's first live work using electronic modification of instrumentally produced sounds. In this work microphones going through filters are attached to a large gong (tam-tam). The technique used is similar to Cage's use of microphones, although the approach is quite different. Like Cage, Stockhausen in another work also used radios: in *Kurzwellen* (1968), although by using short-wave receivers he achieved a global rather than a metropolitan texture. Other techniques used by Stockhausen include extensive use both of ring modulators, and other forms of instrumental intermodulation (*Mixtur*, 1964, and *Mikrophonie II*, 1965) and of complex tape delay systems, as in *Solo* (1965–66). This latter work uses six moveable playback heads, enabling alternation of delay times, and four technical assistants, one of whom switches the playback heads.

Much of the other live electronic music in Europe concentrated on the development of the theatrical aspects of such performances, rather than the application of any particularly complex equipment. Berio's works, even when they are not actually written for the stage, have a strong theatrical element, resulting from the extensive use of voice in performance with tape. Kagel and Nono also tended to concentrate on theatre pieces, using amplification tapes and electronic treatments to heighten social and political themes, rather than create abstract noises and textures. Almost any use of electronics in performance has some element of theatre, especially when combined with improvisation and extensive exploration of unconventional ways of producing sounds. The complex arrays of speakers, mixing-consoles and other bits of electronic paraphernalia also had tremendous fascination for audiences, and added an element of sculpture (a feature later exploited by rock musicians).

This element of almost unintentional mixed-media was seen in the live performance ensembles which developed in several countries. Most of these had a strong element of improvisation, although with differing emphasis and differing degrees of electronic sophistication. Musica Elettronica Viva (most of whose members were American), founded in Rome in 1966, used synthesizers and photocell devices, as well as tapes and other equipment already mentioned. Stockhausen's performing group was the only one to play exclusively the music of one composer, under his own direction. Although much of this was improvisatory, even meditative, the last thought was the composer's, who sat at the mixing desk. The very free improvisation of *Aus den Sieben Tagen* had been anticipated by one of Stockhausen's former assistants, Cornelius Cardew, who was a member of the improvisational group AMM formed in London in 1965. Their use of electronics was relatively simple, and tended to diminish in the late 1960s (leading to the largely non-electronic Scratch Orchestra). Another English ensemble which tended towards an electro-acoustic approach was The Gentle Fire, which included another of Stockhausen's former assistants, Hugh Davies. There was a generally low-tech approach to electronic music in England (notwithstanding the work of Zinovieff and EMS). The English have always liked scientific and technical breakthroughs to have a domestic element about them. In some ways their admiration of a discovery is in proportion to the unsuitable equipment and conditions in which it was produced, as witnessed by the admiration with which Baird's quaint electro-mechanical televisions are regarded. Perhaps it gives a human scale to science; something of this approach is seen in the attitude to music exemplified by Davies's construction of musical instruments out of contact mikes, springs, surplus telephone equipment and so on. Many members of the Scratch Orchestra have used amplified musical toys or other equipment, and although the origins of this are clearly to be found in Cage's works (Music for Amplified Toy Pianos) the effects are generally much easier listening.

Another electronic performance group, Intermodulation, founded by Roger Smalley and Tim Souster in 1970, was more in the European mainstream. Although, as has been pointed out, there was an extra-musical element in all electronic performance it did not in general lead in England to the extension of extra-musical elements to include the active co-operation of artists from other fields. In America the availability of, and enthusiasm for, new performance technology, as well as the existence of a sympathetic movement in the visual arts, led to multi-media collaborations becoming almost *de rigueur*.

Throughout the history of music, avant-garde composers have, from time to time, sought to involve the other arts in their work. It may be that radical developments are often more readily accepted by artists in other fields than by the musical establishment. The invention of opera in late sixteenth-century Florence

The Merce Cunningham Dance Company, formed in 1952 with John Cage as musical director, evolved a form of dance presentation which in Cage's words was 'simply an activity of movement, sound and light'

Japan has been very active in promoting electronic music. At the international **Expo of 1970** in Osaka, several pavilions featured new electronic compositions, the Fujitsu company sponsoring works for their FACOM 270-30 computer

was fostered by the Camerata, a group of composers, both amateur and professional, but also of men of letters and artists. The late nineteenth-century idea of a fusion of all the arts, stemming partly from Wagner, was a dream of painters and poets as well as of musicians. Debussy, arguably the most influential composer of the nineteenth century on twentieth-century composers, acknowledged his relationship with painters and with the Symbolist poets.

It is interesting to note that many of the most controversial premières of this century have been associated with the ballet; *The Rite of Spring*, Satie's *Parade*, the *Ballet mécanique* of George Antheil. This partnership in controversy has continued into the electronic era, most notably in the collaboration of Cage and others with the Merce Cunningham Dance Co. However, the relationship between musicians and artists in every other field – painters, poets, actors, dancers, film-makers, sculptors and architects, as well as scientists – has extended to levels of co-operation undreamt of by Diaghilev.

The modern age has made possible (for the first time) works which not only use all the senses, but which also involve the spectator himself as a part of the creation (or if seen from a different perspective, use music as part of a total environment which has the individual as its centre). The first mixed-media event (or to use the word coined just before the start of the 1960s, 'Happening') in the modern sense was staged by Cage and Cunningham in 1952 at Black Mountain College, North Carolina. Ever since then, the Cunningham Dance Co., with Cage as musical director (usually working with Tudor) and with the collaboration of artists such as Rauschenberg as designers, has constantly been in the vanguard of new and experimental uses of technology.

Particularly interesting has been the development of electronic systems which allow the movements of dancers to be converted directly into music, the dance and the composition being inextricably linked. An example is Cage's *Variations V* (1965), in which rods on stage contain sensors for sounds which are processed and modified in the orchestra pit. Another device developed for the Cunningham Co. (though not by Cage) was the telemetry belt, which converts movement into sound by the use of accelerometers. The signals were sent by radio to the orchestra pit.

The development of equipment which simply by its operation constitutes the composition, or a major part of it, was the particular concern of another composer for the Cunningham Co., Gordon Mumma. An example of his use of such a 'cybersonic' device is in his composition *Hornpipe* (1967), in which a kind of analogue computer attached to the belt of a french horn player analyses and responds to the resonances of the space in which the piece is being performed. (Another work which uses the resonances of the performance space is Lucier's *I am Sitting in a Room*, 1970.) As well as working with Cunningham, Mumma was involved with the ONCE festivals at Ann Arbor, Michigan, organized by Robert Ashley. In 1966 he formed the Sonic Arts Union with other composers, including Ashley, David Berhman and Alvin Lucier, interested in the creation of specialized electronic devices. Some of these works were extremely indeterminate, allowing the technology total artistic licence, for example David Berhman's *Runthrough* (1967), which has no score, only a network of photo cells and electronic sound generators. In this sense they differ from such works as Stockhausen's *Solo*, in which a performer improvises to the effects of the tape delay system.

It seems that in some works American composers used advanced technology to create a parody of the society in which they were living. In Alvin Lucier's *North American Time Capsule* (1967), the composer instructs performers to choose vocal sounds descriptive of contemporary society, using a Vocoder, a digital analytical device used in advanced telecommunications, to process and modify their choices.

Not all their works used space-age gadgetry. Ashley is best known for his composition *The Wolfman* (1964), which uses only a microphone, tape recorder and human voice, amplifying and distorting the voice with electronic bestiality.

Another group of composers continued to work with the relatively familiar resources of the tape recorder, especially the use of tape loops. Terry Riley and Steve Reich have used tape loops to create a rhythmic excitement which borders on rock. LaMonte Young has used tapes to extend compositions for several hours, with barely perceptible changes.

The experimental spirit of live electronic music in America initiated by Cage continually produced new music from both high and low technology, not least in Cage's own works.

The exploration of the unexploited sounds of the piano, begun with the prepared piano pieces of the late 1930s, continued with the

Winter Music and *Variations II* (and also at a slight tangent with the *Music for Amplified Toy Pianos* – an ironic comment on the status of the piano. The basic technical resource was amplification – both of the expected piano sound and of the normally inaudible sounds within the instrument.

Other works of Cage, for example *HPSCHD* (1967–9, in collaboration with Hiller), use more extravagant resources, in this case seven amplified harpsichords, up to fifty-one tapes and, in the process of composition, a computer.

David Tudor, who performed nearly all of Cage's pieces, tended in his own works towards a complex multi-media approach. (He also developed a very large number of customized performance devices.) His *Bandoneon!* uses music generated by the Argentinian accordion-like bandoneon, together with lights, television, lasers and other theatrical and environmental elements. Another work, *Rainforest*, uses specially constructed 'Instrumental loudspeakers', which by using the differing resonance of different materials become instruments in their own rights.

The work of Morton Subotnick in San Francisco, in collaboration with synthesizer designer Donald Buchla and visual artist Anthony Martin, was interesting particularly because of the influence it had on rock events of the psychedelic era. The use of synthesizers and other electronics combined with the use of light projected through liquids was to find echoes in rock for many years. More directly involved with rock, though less immediately influential, was Warhol's mixed media event of 1966, The Exploding Plastic Inevitable, which used the rock group The Velvet Underground (in the same way, one suspects, as some novel technical resource might have been used).

Virtually every technical resource does appear to have been used in America during the late 1960s. To mention just a few examples, Illinois composer Salvatore Martirano has used a gas-masked performer, his voice modulated to castrato pitch by a helium atmosphere to declaim the Gettysburg address, in *L's G.A.* (1968). In Max Neuhaus's *Drive-in Music* (1967), weather-sensing radio transmitters performed to passing motorists on their car radios. Other sources for sounds used in musical compositions have included listeners phoning in to a radio station to have voices treated, and brain waves registered by electroencephalographs attached to the heads of performers (David Rosenbloom's Bio-feedback Quartet).

With the increasing availability of television, video and lasers, etc., several composers have collaborated with visual artists and technicians in this field. Cage, Tudor, Cross and Korean artist Nam June Paik are leading figures, although such is the cost and technical complexity of the resources required that most video/laser works involve collaboration between many people.

At the ultimate extreme of multi-media events have been the works or environments specially created for a particular architectural and spatial setting, usually at World Fairs or similar exhibitions. The first of these was for the Philips Pavilion at the Brussels Exhibition in 1958. This was created jointly by the architect Le Corbusier, composer Edgard Varèse and the architect and composer Iannis Xenakis. Varèse, in the face of considerable opposition from Philips, was chosen by Le Corbusier to write a piece of music to be played through 350 loudspeakers in the specially designed building. During the performance of this, *Le Poème électronique,* images chosen by Le Corbusier were projected on to the concrete walls.

Xenakis, who had been responsible for the design of the building, in fact, deriving parabolas and other shapes mathematically from music, also wrote a piece specially for the pavilion, *Concret PH.* Whereas Varèse has derived his material from a wide range of emotive sounds, Xenakis used only the sound of smouldering charcoal. The effect on audiences was both overwhelming and controversial.

Twelve years later, the Pepsi-Cola pavilion at the Expo '70 exhibition at Osaka represented the advances in technology with a presentation involving among other things an artificially generated water vapour cloud, a sculpture which tracked the sun projecting a beam of sunlight into a geodesic dome which contained a computer-controlled sound and light environment (with 32 inputs and 37 speakers). Outside were sound-emitting floats which constantly moved and changed direction when touched. The pavilion was the result of collaboration between many artists. Many other environments involving sound and other elements have been built, including the German Music Pavilion in Osaka (1970), for which Stockhausen wrote music.

A melancholy extension of the idea of a sound environment is the piped Muzak which replaces bad drains as the pervasive nuisance of industrialized society. (Ironically its progenitor was Cahill, the pioneer of electronic music.)

MULTI-MEDIA ROCK

Rock and roll, with its reliance on the electric guitar and microphone, has always been a live electronic genre. Being in general capitalists as well as artists, rock musicians have always provided an enthusiastic and affluent market for new inventions, without the inherent conservatism of the classical establishment.

From the late 1960s on, rock musicians began to become more aware of developments in the avant-garde, at the same time as a tremendous acceleration in new technological developments took place. One result was the monster rock concerts of the seventies, with lights, lasers, thousands of watts of amplification, special effects and a stage full of thousands of pounds' worth of high technology and instruments. Another result was a genuine fusion of rock with aspects of the low-tech avant-garde.

The multi-media rock event developed directly from the art events and 'happenings' which took place in San Francisco and New York, starting in the early 1960s. Ideas from Subotnick's collaborations with visual artists at the Trip Festivals in San Francisco were taken up by rock musicians such as Zappa and The Grateful Dead, and given a shot of drug culture to become the pleasure gardens of the psychedelic era. (LSD was still legal when Tom Wolfe documented the period in *The Electric Kool-Aid Acid Test* in the mid-sixties.)

Making no concessions whatever to love, peace and 'good vibes' was the New York group The Velvet Underground, which toured America as part of Andy Warhol's mixed-media show, The Exploding Plastic Inevitable, in 1966. Overtly influenced by avant-garde music, their hard, urban sound (which was to prove extremely influential in spite of being commercially unacceptable) utilized electric viola and generous amounts of feedback on the guitar.

When the lights were down, the two major innovations of psychedelic rock were feedback, and the introduction of new instruments such as synthesizers. Feedback is the result of a signal from a guitar being picked up by the guitar again, after it has come from the loudspeakers, causing a kind of modulation which produces a sustained note with some distortion and strongly reinforced high harmonics. Enormously increased amounts of amplification made the use of feedback possible. Although it had been used by the avant-garde (for example in Behrman's *Wavetrain*, 1966), it

Four angles on a German rock concert given by Roxy Music. *(Below):* Phil Manzanera, guitarist. The pedal board for producing a variety of effects is almost as complex as that on an organ console.
(Left): A general view of the arena, showing the complexity of equipment needed for such a performance

(Far left): A view of the stage during the concert. *(Immediately left):* The technician operating the controls is placed in the middle of the auditorium, in order to have the optimum vantage point

was primarily exploited by rock musicians. At low levels, combined with fuzz pedals and wah-wah, it contributed to the sustained and highly emotional sound of the late sixties exemplified by the playing of Eric Clapton. Used overtly, it could produce electronic effects closer to the ring modulators and other devices of the avant-garde, as in the devastating version of 'The Star-Spangled Banner' played by Hendrix at Woodstock.

Very high levels of amplification could produce distortion and feedback in other instruments, notably organ, a feature exploited by various other groups such as The Soft Machine, and by the organist Keith Emerson. Emerson, whose theatrical excesses with the Hammond include sticking daggers in the keyboard and allowing the instrument to crash heavily on to the stage (creating a loud, explosive reverberation) also pioneered stage use of the Moog synthesizer.

By the early 1970s, the pattern of the monster, touring rock band had been established. Equipped with PA systems developed from those used at the giant festivals of the sixties, and financed by a boom in record sales (especially of albums), the major groups set out with fleets of articulated lorries carrying the equipment to build night by night a multi-media show of formidable proportions. Groups vied with each other to stay ahead in the league

of technological overkill: Led Zeppelin with a huge PA and lasers; Emerson, Lake & Palmer with a revolving drum kit and a complete symphony orchestra individually amplified with contact mikes; Funkadelic, its members emerging in glittering space suits from a rocket; and the undisputed masters of the rock concert as multi-media show, Pink Floyd. Having their origins firmly in the psychedelic era, and the first group in England to carry a light-show, Pink Floyd developed lights, special effects, the use of tapes and multi-directional speaker set-ups to a new level of sophistication. Their 1980 shows for *The Wall* involved the group playing in front of and behind a huge wall, which was constructed (and destroyed) during the performance. Extensive use was made of pre-recorded tapes and speakers positioned around the hall, as well as complicated lights and projections. These concerts represent the most ambitious touring multi-media events yet attempted.

Instrument manufacturers were not slow to realize the market potential of the new rock. Although many of the instruments developed were synthesizers or organs, there were one or two interesting hybrids. The Mellotron (used by King Crimson in 1969 and later by many

Pink Floyd in their mixed-media presentation 'The Wall', which was assembled and demolished during performance

groups, including Roxy Music) was a keyboard instrument using pre-recorded tapes. In effect it was a multiple tape recorder, each key activating a tape. Instrumental sounds were on the tapes, the flutes and strings having a particularly distinctive, eerie quality (heard on The Beatles' 'Strawberry Fields for Ever'). Other sounds could be recorded and added at will.

Another aspect of high-technology rock was the electrification of acoustic instruments. Partly as an attempt to be heard against the massive sounds emerging from guitars and keyboards, sax and flute players (and a few violinists and other instrumentalists) attached contact mikes, or 'bugs' to their instruments. This encouraged experiment with effects pedals and other devices. Although most of these are made for guitar, various players – King Curtis and Eddie Harris for example – pioneered the use of wah-wah, octave dividers and other effects on electric sax. Miles Davis has also used electronic effects on the trumpet. Electrified acoustic pianos for stage use, notably the Yamaha, have continued the quest for perfect amplified pianos started long ago with the Neo-Bechstein. An electro-acoustic device much used in the late seventies was the voice box (well known through its use by Peter Frampton), a simple arrangement of tubing with which a guitarist could modulate the guitar sound with his mouth, producing a 'talking' effect. The effect of a Vocoder, a much more complex piece of equipment, is similar.

Another more recent feature of rock on stage is the use of devices such as limiters, noise gates and digital delay systems – previously considered exclusively studio equipment. Particularly in areas using tape loops and similar effects, rock and art music have occasionally come together. The collaboration of Velvet Underground member John Cale with Terry Riley is an example, and the performances of the German rock group Can (which includes two pupils of Stockhausen) also bordered on the rock-art frontier.

By the 1980s, rock music, though not quite equalling the experimental originality of the avant-garde in its use of electronic equipment, had nevertheless applied it to a wider range of styles and with a more direct appeal to the listeners' emotions. It had also caught up with – and maybe exceeded – the avant-garde in its use of the most modern technology, both in performance and in the studio. Inevitably, for all modern musicians this has come to mean digital technology, computers and micro-chips.

COMPUTERS

There has been considerable confusion over the role of computers in electronic music, reflecting the general mixture of awe and mistrust with which they are viewed in society at large, now that they occupy the niche in the technical pantheon once vacated by steam to make way for electricity.

There have been several computer-like features in electronic music and its antecedents; from musical boxes and player pianos to the RCA synthesizer (which used the same punched paper rolls). There was also the Bell Telephone Laboratories' Vocoder (which so impressed Meyer-Eppler). The use of true computers in the generation of electronic music, although intermittently exciting, has not been crucial to its understanding. But it seems probable that, in the near future, knowledge of computer techniques will come to be vital to an understanding of the new music.

Computers have three main functions in music: passive, for control or storage; active, as a part of a compositional process; and also as a means of actually creating sounds by using one of the computer programmes specially developed for that purpose. It is important to understand the operation of the two types of computer, digital and analogue, in order to explain this.

Computers are machines that process information by counting. Information put in at one end appears at the other in a new form. This may be 2 + 2 appearing as 4, or it may be information contained in a keyboard appearing as a note. The distinction between analogue and digital devices lies in the way the information is represented and/or counted. In an analogue device one unit represents another by analogy, whereas in a digital device everything is reduced to numbers, each number representing a small but finite quantity. To take an example (which is neither musical nor computerized), a traditional watch face is an analogue device in which the position of the hands represents time by analogy: a movement of ninety degrees represents the passage of fifteen minutes. A digital watch, however, tells time by counting: fifteen minutes is represented as 0.15. A voltage-controlled synthesizer is an analogue device in which changes in voltage represent notes. But in general, the use of computers in music means the use of digital computers (although a digital computer can be linked to an analogue device by means of a digital-to-analogue converter).

The main features of digital computers are tremendous speed and complete accuracy. The drawback is that since any phenomenon is represented as a series of separate numbers, any continuous process has to be reduced to a series of jumps. In practice, these can be so close together that they are heard as continuous. Digital recording (which is rapidly becoming the norm for classical recording and for the upper echelons of rock) illustrates this point. In a traditional magnetic tape recording, the tape – with its pattern of magnetic impulses – is an analogy of the music that has been recorded on it. Each passing note is represented continuously by the changing relative values of its component harmonics. In digital recording, the relative strength of every frequency in every note being sounded at any particular moment is represented by a number. In order that these numbers can be converted into sound, they have to go through a digital-to-analogue converter. (The main advantages of digital recording are that there is no tape noise build up; that a whole piece is available for almost instantaneous replay without waiting for rewinding; and editing is also extremely accurate.) A normal sound-mixing desk is used, although with the use of the computer memory, mixes can be made stage by stage with only minor adjustments. In a fully computerized studio, recording, editing and mixing facilities are all part of the same unit, making obsolete the tape recorder and editing block.

Digital tape recording is a comparatively recent application of the technology (the first commercial digital tape was produced in 1977). Computers were first used to generate sounds – by the reverse process, in which particular frequencies were programmed in specific relative strengths – at the Bell Telephone Laboratories in 1957. One of the earliest practical applications of digital analysis was in the Vocoder, which converted speech to digital information in order to transmit it over telephone lines. Even earlier than this, computers had been used in their other role: as partners in the composition of music.

Because a computer is an extremely complex device, the way in which information is presented to it affects the way in which it is processed, and so affects the end product. This process is called programming, and can affect the output of the computer to the extent that several composers have felt it a legitimate means of composition: to programme a computer in such a way that it can complete a compositional process. The first composer to use computers in this way was Lejaren Hiller at the University of Illinois in 1957, producing the *Illiac Suite*. The computer produced only the score for this work, which was for string quartet, using numbers which represented pitch, duration and instrumentation.

Another composer who used computers in composition was Xenakis. Mathematician and architect, as well as musician, he had by about 1959 evolved a method of composition using probability theory statistics and various game procedures, although without recourse to computers. This he called stochastic music, and it is very broadly based on the tendency of a large number of random alternatives to move towards a determinate end. (The word 'stochastic' comes from the Greek for 'target', and was first used by the eighteenth-century mathematician Bernoulli, who developed the law of large numbers.) From the early 1960s, computers were used to perform these myriad operations at the speed of light.

Interestingly enough, this was also the effect in performance of the music produced by chance operations (called aleatoric music) by John Cage and others, though Cage's music allowed much greater freedom to the performer than did that of Xenakis. Cage, incidentally, used computers in the work *HPSCHD*, which he wrote jointly with Lejaren Hiller.

The computer can also function as a highly efficient control mechanism for an analogue synthesizer. An early digital device on synthesizers was the sequencer, though this is a far more simple device than real computer mechanism. A sequencer repeats a relatively short sequence of notes (or any other synthesizer function), usually up to about thirty; these can be altered in time or pitch, and the steady, characterless repetition has been effectively used many times.

A real synthesizer can do much more than this, controlling and altering pitch, duration, timbre attack and any other function for as long as is required. The Synthi 100 made by EMS was one of the first and best known larger synthesizers to include a computer. Obviously a computer used in this way can be a great aid to composition, since ideas can be replayed and edited as desired.

The synthesizer which combines all the functions of the computer in one system is the Fairlight CMI, available commercially since 1979.

The Fairlight Synthesizer can analyse and reassemble sounds at any pitch. The operator is selecting peaks and troughs from four wave patterns

The CMI (Computer Musical Instrument), which is manufactured in Sydney, is entirely digital: sounds are generated, stored and processed by means of a computer. While it is not the only digital computer synthesizer, the CMI does have several features which make it particularly exciting in use. One of these is the ability to 'sample' natural sounds through a microphone or tape recorder. These are then analysed digitally into their harmonic components, and can then be regenerated – with altered pitch and duration if required. This means that musical scales can be made out of any sound: speech, for example, percussive sounds or animal noises. A display screen is used to show, among other things, the graphic representation of waveforms. With the use of a light-pen, this can function like an oscilloscope in reverse; a waveform can be drawn on to the screen and the synthesizer will play it. Since there are no switches, knobs or patch cords, the light-pen is also used to programme information. The use of digital waveform analysis, stored in micro-chips, has also been applied to inexpensive domestic organs by Casio, better known for their calculators.

It has been pointed out that the only thing to be said about the music of the future is that it hasn't happened yet. Instruments only really survive through the music written for them; relatively few of the dozens of electronic instruments invented since the turn of the century are in current use. But instrument technology is developing at an ever-increasing speed, which even the most optimistic would think allows composers little time to write enduring classics. Only ten years before the Fairlight CMI became available, the author purchased an EMS VCS3 (Putney). Having just become available, this represented an amazingly compact and versatile electronic instrument for musicians who were not otherwise able to assemble the numerous bits of equipment required. Ten years before that there were only two or three synthesizers in the world, and only a few electronic studios – expensive and complicated laboratory equipment available only to a specialized minority. Such a decadal approach could be taken further, to the time ten years before that when tape recorders themselves were a novelty.

The violin, which appeared in the sixteenth century, did not make its full impact on composition until a century later. In half that time electronics has completely changed the way we hear music. Partly this is through new sounds; partly it is through the universality of the loudspeaker, 'the streetwalker of music', with whom familiarity appears to have bred respect. The technology is with us to stay. The music which has been created using the technology is the subject of the next part of this book.

The oscillograph of a symphony orchestra is extremely complex, yet the ear is able to distinguish individual instruments

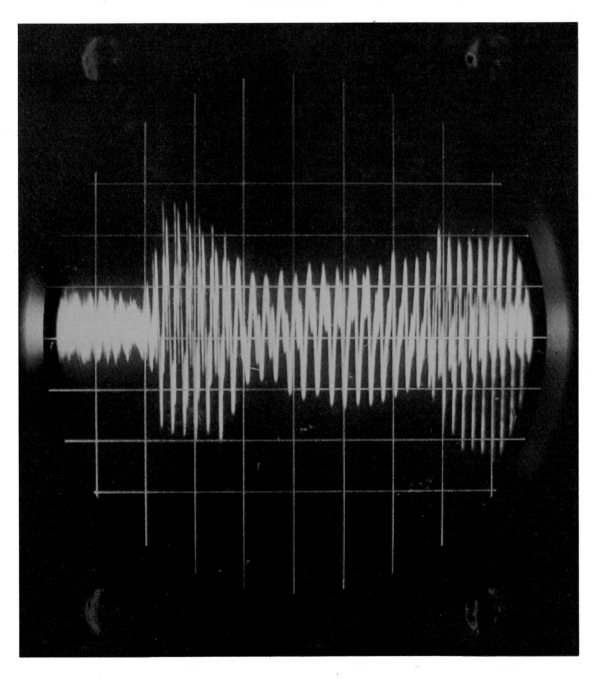

THE MUSIC

The history of music specifically written for electronic instruments extends back little more than forty years. The aesthetic and judgemental problems that its creation poses for composers are immense: the acoustic range and potential volume, for example, are virtually limitless. The frequent absence of human performers and the task of evolving suitable notations are likewise formidable. This section, therefore, must also deal with the reactions of composers to these factors. Rock music, too, though something of a hybrid, has developed a musical language that is highly dependent on electronic and electro-acoustic instruments – though it largely eschews the problem of notation. Popular and 'art' music were never further apart than in the decade following the Second World War, but if they share a common ground it is in the field of electronics. This fusion, now increasingly apparent, is also discussed in the following section.

ELECTRONICS IN THE ORCHESTRA

Looking back at the use of electronic instruments, it is apparent that most developments took place at extreme poles of the musical scene. On the one hand by members of an avant-garde creating music of almost unprecedented incomprehensibility and on the other by the most popular musicians in history. This paradox is reflected in a discussion of the music which has resulted; a task which is in any case made difficult by the shortness of the historical perspective. In scarcely two decades from the early 1940s to the late 1960s, the language of music was extended both in the range of sounds used, in new musical forms and in radically new methods of composition and performance, with a variety and speed which not even the dramatic developments of the earlier part of the century had suggested. But whereas the compositions and ideas of Cage, Stockhausen and others were too obscure for general acceptance (even up to the time of writing), at the same time a new musical style was developing which could not be ignored: rock and roll. Later these two seemingly contradictory

movements crossed over here and there. Nevertheless some works will be discussed principally because of the challenging or exciting ideas which lie behind them, others because they are popular.

Although electronics have increasingly been used to create music which could not be produced any other way, most electronic music developed initially from the existing musical background. This is seen in the way in which the performance instruments of the twenties and thirties were first used.

From early in the nineteenth century, an increasing concern with tone colour had led to the expansion of the orchestra with various 'occasional' instruments (some of which became permanent members). These included newly invented instruments such as the cor anglais and the saxophone, specially constructed instruments like the Wagner Tuba, or the wooden trumpet used in the third act of *Tristan*, and an enormous range of new and newly discovered percussion instruments, ranging from the exoticism of large oriental gongs to the ludicrous wind machine in Strauss's Alpine Symphony. By the early twentieth century, orchestration had come to be considered almost a separate art. Orchestral players were required to extend their technique to produce new timbres and textures, a feature of modern instrumental playing which has increased rather than diminished since the widespread use of electronics, with such requirements as microtonal playing from string players and complex harmonics from woodwind players.

The first serious composers to use electronic instruments used them in this occasional manner: as a new voice within the orchestra or as a solo instrument with a new range, timbre and flexibility of articulation. Of the new instruments of the twenties and thirties the trautonium and the ondes martenot were the two for which a firm repertoire was established. The theremin, although it later made a distinctive contribution to film scores, was less used by composers in the classical tradition. The telharmonium, in spite of its inventor's high aspiration (and the visionary enthusiasm of Busoni), never played anything much more than salon music.

The main disadvantage of the theremin was that it could not be precisely pitched, having no keyboard or indication for specific notes. Although the established composers who wrote for the trautonium and the ondes, notably Hindemith, Varèse, Jolivet and Messiaen, made liberal use of its capacity for glissandi and vibrato effects, they wrote within the conventional modern musical idioms of the time. The notation too was conventional, with the parts normally written on a single stave in the treble clef with considerable use of octave signs.

· Hindemith's Concertino for Trautonium and Strings, written in 1931, is the earliest of full-scale works for the new electronic instruments, showing how its composer had an approach to composition which not only included the respect for traditions of craftmanship for which he is well known but also welcomed the new (something also seen in his experiments with variable-speed gramophone turntables).

Jolivet's Concerto for Ondes Martenot and Orchestra, although a later work, dating from 1952, shows the same traditional approach. A difficult virtuoso piece, pitting the ondes against a large orchestra (a situation in which the possibility of increasing the volume at will must have been very useful), it featured cadenzas which must have tested the technique of even so experienced a performer as Madame Martenot, to whom it was dedicated.

Messiaen also uses the ondes as a solo instrument in his Turangalîla Symphony, the work in which the instrument probably has its most important place in the repertory. Use is made of all the main sounds of the instrument, especially the 'metal' tone which is reinforced by a small gong in the resonator, and which can produce loud – even terrifying – noises, and the more delicate sounds produced by the 'palm', the set of sympathetic strings like a lyre which reinforce various overtones. The overwhelming effect of Messiaen's use of the ondes martenot, particularly in a work as richly scored as is the Turangalila Symphony, is as startling as it is effective, and must have been shattering when the work was heard in a time before electronic sounds had become commonplace. At times it plays with force, adding a fierce and strange power to the climaxes. At other times it is used more delicately, as in the second movement, the Chant d'amour, where it is both unearthly and sensual, as when doubling the strings an octave up, sounding half-way between a disembodied female voice and a mysterious flute. (Messiaen indicates throughout the score most carefully the specific tone that he requires.)

Varèse used two ondes martenot in his Ecuatorial (1934). In this work (which uses a pre-Colombian Mayan chant as its text) the ondes take up from the high woodwind playing, sliding ethereal notes higher than any human voice can take them – at one point reaching E above the top note of the piano.

Varèse used the ondes as an entirely new instrument and although he advocated its use for microtones, this was done by Messiaen more thoroughly in his Deux Monodies for ondes martenot (1938). Boulez also wrote a Quartet for ondes martenot (1945–46), since withdrawn. Other composers also used electronic instruments to perform parts not possible with conventional instruments. Percy Grainger used four theremins to perform Free Music in 1935, and another great innovator, Henry Cowell, used a 'rhythmicon' – specially constructed for him by Theremin – to perform rhythmic structures too complex for human performers.

After the war some composers used existing electronic instruments in combination with other instruments: for example, Berio's use of the electric guitar in Chemins I/II (1970–72) or Boulez's use of the same instrument in Domaines (1961–69), but these fit in more with the idea of electronic instruments as an addition to the existing instrumental line-up for tone colour than as electronic music. That phrase had come to have a much more specific meaning by the start of the 1950s.

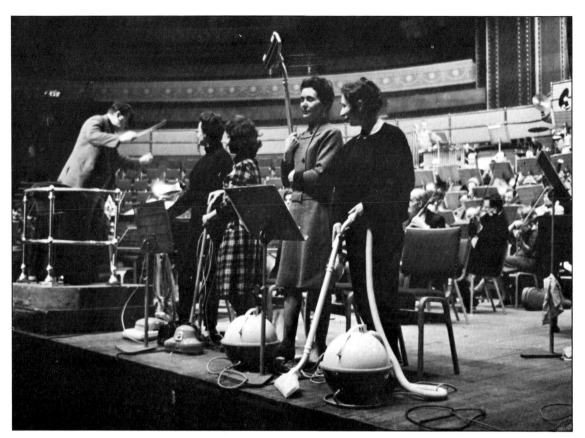

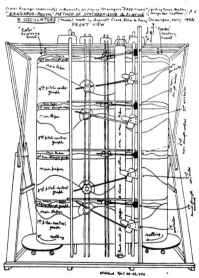

Paul Hindemith, celebrated German composer, and teacher of Friedrich Trautwein. Although not usually associated with electronic music, Hindemith in fact wrote several pieces (including a small concerto) for his pupil's invention, the trautonium

Olivier Messiaen. He delights in using exotic sounds in his scores. In rejecting the noise-generating machines of the Futurists, he complains, 'Why have you slavishly produced what is already commonplace and boring in our lives?'

(Top): A light-hearted view of electronic music at a 'Hoffnung' concert in London. *(Above):* A remarkable performance machine was this one designed by Burnett Cross and the Australian composer Percy Grainger in 1952

TAPE MUSIC

It was a device not normally thought of as an instrument at all, the tape recorder, which made electronic music possible. Although developed by 1935, the magnetic tape recorder was not generally available until 1950. In 1948 Pierre Schaeffer produced some studies in what he called *musique concrète*, using gramophone records of such sound effects as train noises. These were manipulated by changing the speed, superimposing one sound on another, and so on. A concert of these was broadcast in October 1948 as a 'concert of noises'. As a result of the interest generated, the French radio network (RTF) gave Schaeffer more studio facilities, including the use of tape recorders. Schaeffer, in collaboration with one of the young musicians who was excited by the possibilities of the new medium, Pierre Henry, produced the first extended *musique concrète* composition, *Symphonie pour un homme seul*, which was premièred in 1950. In 1951 the Groupe de musique concrète was set up at the Paris radio station, the first electronic studio.

The Parisian school of *musique concrète* had its antecedents in the noise concerts of Russolo and the Futurists, dating from the period of the First World War, and in such works as Antheil's *Ballet mécanique*. But whereas the Futurist *intonarumori* (noise makers) only simulated the dramatic mechanical noises of modern life (rather unconvincingly, to judge from the admittedly poor recordings of them that exist) using wooden levers, membranes and string hidden inside boxes, and while Antheil (and Satie in *Parade*) had to use actual aeroplane propellers and sirens, the composers of *musique concrète* were able to use actual sounds recorded in the field, which could be processed and organized at will in the calm of the studio.

It was this process of organization in the studio which produced in *musique concrète* the first examples of an entirely new form of music, created in its definitive form directly by the composer without the traditional process of writing a score to be performed and interpreted by other musicians. It was this absence of an abstract representation of the composer's thoughts which was meant by 'concrete' music, although the term is more generally used to refer to music which uses 'everyday' sounds rather than sounds generated electronically.

The concept of pure electronic music was the product of several composers who initially used the RTF studio, Boulez, Stockhausen and (to a lesser extent) the man who was their teacher, Messiaen. The main difference between them and the composers of the Paris school was in their approach to musical form and in particular the application of serialism requiring the precision of sounds generated electronically. Early electronic works by Boulez and Stockhausen were thus related to earlier pre-electronic works. The concrete composers felt theirs to be an entirely new field of music, and developed forms around the timbres of the sounds and of the emotions they evoked. Although Schaeffer acknowledged some debt to the Futurists, this was really only in respect of their use of noises as a basis for musical performances. The pre-electronic noise works were in any case pretty feeble bits of music, and relied almost entirely on their shock value. If there was any influence

(Right): **Pierre Henry,** pioneer of electronic music.
(Below): **The Bride Stripped Bare by her Bachelors, Even** by the Dadaist Marcel Duchamp

from art movements of the earlier part of the century, it was more likely the collages of the Dadaists and others, for many pieces of *musique concrète* were musical collages. One thing that Schaeffer achieved was to impose some sort of unity and discipline on his works by limiting the sound source to one particular sound or group of sounds. This is seen in the titles of them (all of which are called Études): from the *Étude aux chemins de fer*, using the sounds of trains, or the *Étude aux casseroles*, using sounds derived from saucepan lids. He later classified sound sources with great precision in his book *Traité des objets misicaux* (1966). Unfortunately Schaeffer seems to have got bogged down with this approach, producing a lot of short compositions demonstrating the variety of tonal resources available to anyone who was interested in turning their everyday environment into a musical instrument, rather than pursuing any particular musical goal. His aim was not the iconoclastic acceptance of all sounds proposed by John Cage, but rather a belief in the transforming power of the tape studio.

Schaeffer's collaboration with Henry produced a sequence of works using the techniques of *musique concrète* which were musically more interesting. The *Symphonie pour un homme seul* was the first of these: it used a wide range of recorded sounds as its basic material, including many derived from the human voice. The human condition is reflected in eleven short, contrasting movements, some erotic, some pathetic, others more abstract. Another major work to use tape in the early period, Varèse's *Déserts* (1949–54), also reflects the existential tone of the period in a more sombre fashion. Varèse wrote 'deserts mean to me not only the physical deserts of sand, sea, mountains and snow, of outer space, of empty city streets . . . but also that remote inner space no telescope can reach, where man is alone in a world of mystery and essential loneliness'. Tape music was uniquely able to express this most twentieth-century preoccupation. The three tape sections of *Déserts* are interpolated between orchestral passages. The first has an industrial quality suggesting the sound of heavy machinery, while the later sections are weirder and more abstract. Varèse's other major tape work, the *Poème électronique* (1958), also uses a very wide range of sounds as its basic material. Described by the composer as 'a protest against inquisition in every form' it compresses great emotional power into a mere eight minutes. Originally written for perfor-

mance in the Philips Pavilion at the Brussels World Fair, it has a strong sense of structure, of 'organized sound', which makes it more than an aural collage.

Cage's early tape work, the *Williams Mix* (1952), which can be considered the first American example of *musique concrète*, is an anarchic assembly of a very wide range of sound sources, randomly and disturbingly put together with many edits. Most composers however took their lead from Schaeffer and approached the formal and musical possibilities of *musique concrète* using a deliberately limited basic sound source. Iannis Xenakis both extended the length and structural basis of tape compositions and observed the strictest limitations on the source material in his *Concret PH* (also written in 1958 for performance in the Philips Pavilion). The sole sound source is the crackling of smouldering charcoal, although the composer was applying mathematical and architectural principles in which the slow changes of density of sound masses were meant to create great sweeps, the hyperbolic paraboloids referred to in the title. This work shows very clearly another aspect of electronic music that was to assume great importance, that of performance in a spatial dimension. This was clearly not a new idea, even in an overt form (as the music written by Giovanni Gabrieli for St Mark's in Venice in the seventeenth cen-

tury shows), however, almost infinite control over the relative volume of several speakers gave electronic composers an unprecedented freedom, subtlety and power to create three-dimensional sonic structures. In the case of the Philips Pavilion there were 350 individual speakers and, since the building had been designed by Xenakis, there was a particularly intimate relationship of music to the architectural space. (The pavilion, which had been constructed under the direction of Le Corbusier, primarily as a performance space for Varèse's *Poème électronique*, has unfortunately been demolished.) The use of loudspeakers positioned around the audience or the extensive use of stereo effects on recordings is frequently essential to the understanding of the electronic composers' intentions. A relatively insignificant sound can assume great power and mystery when heard as truly three-dimensional, a lesson learned long ago by the builders of temples and cathedrals.

Both in Europe and America composers continued to be fascinated by the mysterious riches of sound which could be obtained from quite familiar objects through the transforming power of the studio. The pioneers of tape music in the USA, Luening and Ussachevsky, created several highly influential works using traditional musical instruments as the source, and little more than a tape recorder and micro-

(Top left): **Edgard Varèse** in 1910. *(Far left):* A projection taken from **Le Poème électronique**, one of the first productions which used light-projected images with recorded tape. *(Near left):* The famous **Philips pavilion** (now demolished) built by Le Corbusier, where *Le Poème électronique* had its first performance at the Brussels Expo in 1958, together with other experimental works

phone. Ussachevsky used a piano in his *Sonic Contours* which, by changing the speed of the tape, was transformed into deep gong-like sounds when slowed down or bright metallic sounds when speeded up. Another effect much used in tape music was the sustained organ-like sound obtained by cutting off the attack of a note. Luening used a flute as the basis for two compositions which he himself has described as 'impressionistic, virtuoso pieces', *Fantasy in Space* and *Low Speed*. As the title suggests the latter piece explores the sound obtained from the flute when taken down to below its natural range, though the sound was also modified with a kind of reverberation device and tape echo. Although the form of these pieces was free and improvisatory in character Luening also wrote a piece, *Invention*, which used a twelve-tone row, paralleling the concern with serial structure of Boulez and Stockhausen in Europe, and Babbitt in the USA. All of these pieces were premièred at a concert at the Museum of Modern Art in New York in 1952, a venue which was perhaps indicative of the interest in electronic music shown by the art world rather than the musical establishment.

The 'classical' approach to *musique concrète* was followed for some years by various composers in America. Notable examples are Canadian Hugh Le Caine's *Dripsody* (1955) produced from the sound of a single splash, and Turkish-American composer Ilhan Mimaroglu's *Bowery Bum* (1964), which uses rubber bands as its sole sound source.

Another approach to the use of tape as a means of musical composition was the use of the human voice, generally concentrating on the sounds produced by speech rather than the notes produced by singing. Henry, who had already used speech, laughter, breathing, etc., in the *Symphonie pour un homme seul* produced a work, *Vocalise* (1952), using only the sound 'Ah'. Italian composer Luciano Berio used a longer text, an excerpt from Joyce's *Ulysses*, in his influential composition *Thema* (sub-titled *Omaggio a Joyce*), written in 1958. Even though the words are used in a way which gradually sacrifices meaning to sound, the form of the piece is (more or less) determined by the text with considerable dramatic effect as the female voice moves gradually into unintelligibility. A later work (written like *Thema* for the soprano Cathy Berberian), *Visage* (1961), uses non-verbal vocal sounds electronically treated, extending the 'stream of consciousness' approach of the earlier Joyce piece.

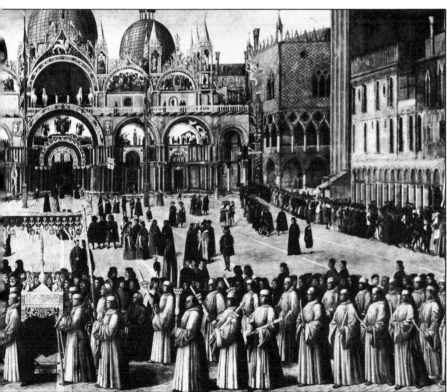

(Top left): **The Museum of Modern Art, New York** (known affectionately as MOMA), where Otto Luening and Vladimir Ussachevsky gave the first performance of taped music, *Sonic Contours* in 1952

(Above): Cathy Berberian, renowned both as an interpreter of avant garde music and a composer in her own right

St Mark's Cathedral, Venice. The splendid basilica, with its two organs and organ lofts, was the scene of some of the first excursions into multidirectional sound

71

THE ELECTRONIC STUDIO: STOCKHAUSEN

The development of a different approach to the use of the studio in electronic music was to have a far-reaching effect on all forms of electronic composition, although only after a largely illusory conflict had been resolved.

In 1952, a short while after the studio was established in Paris, an electronic studio was set up at the radio station in Cologne. The approach to the creation of electronic music was, however, very different. The main theoretical basis of compositions was serialism, an extension of the use of a tone row by the twelve-tone composers of the second Viennese school, who arranged notes in a 'series', no one of which could be repeated until all the others had been sounded. A group of young post-war composers, notably Boulez and Stockhausen (under the influence of the music of Webern, Messiaen and the teaching of the first director of the studio, Herbert Eimert), developed a belief in the almost divine value of such organization applied not only to pitch but to all the other parameters of music; dynamics, duration, rhythm and timbre. Such precise values could only be fully achieved with the use of sounds all generated electronically; hence the music of the Cologne school came to be known as 'pure' electronic music.

Stockhausen immediately began to work on two Studies in which all the sounds were produced and modified entirely by electronics, even attempting to produce timbre by the incredibly pedantic method of superimposing pure sine tones at the pitch and relative loudness of the desired notes of the harmonic series. Apart from being extremely time consuming, this approach to timbre control was not entirely successful, and the pure electronic approach was relatively short-lived. For a few years there was lively discussion in electronic circles as to the relative merits of the 'concrete' approach or the purely electronic approach. This began to fade away later in the 1950s, especially after Stockhausen began to use both vocal and electronic sounds in his *Gesang der Jünglinge* (1955–56), and instruments with a varied range of techniques of processing sounds electronically in *Kontakte* (1958–60). Such a distinction never arose in America, where many different approaches to electronic music developed simultaneously, or in Italy, the other major

European country for electronic music.

Stockhausen's compositions from the later part of the decade are perhaps the first works in which one feels a composer is working with total confidence and freedom in an entirely new medium, and they confirmed his growing status as the leading figure in European electronic music. Unlike several other prominent composers such as the Transylvanian Ligeti, who produced one or two works in the new medium and then turned back towards an instrumental tradition, Stockhausen continued to use electronics as a major part of his activities for the next two decades.

Much of his work is concerned with the inter-relationships between the physical elements that make a musical event, and is an attempt to create a unity and interaction between these elements. This is what lay behind the concern to relate pitch, rhythm, timbre and volume serially in the *Studie I*. Electronics enabled him to take these relationships with a precision far beyond the audible. (Cage, with a certain amount of irony, quoted Stockhausen on this as saying, 'It makes me feel so good to know I am on the right track'.) Another relationship of great importance is that between speech and music. A detailed study of phonetics lay behind this interest, which is most obviously evidenced in the *Gesang der Jünglinge*, which uses the sound of a boy's voice reciting the words from the *Benedicite*, said to have been sung from within the burning fiery furnace. The words are broken down into parts of varying length, mixed with electronic sounds, and given a spatial dimension by the use of several loudspeakers. The results of this interest are heard in several other works, however, including some not involving vocals. In *Mikrophonie I*, which explores the sonorities obtained by moving microphones around a tam-tam, several of the sounds obtained seem strangely vocal. This work also shows another aspect of composition that was to become enormously important: that of the relationship between performers. This is often to be a symbol or metaphor of the physical relationship between sounds. Whereas Stockhausen's earliest electronic works had been precisely notated, indeed they were the first electronic works to have a 'score', by the time of *Mikrophonie I* in 1964 only the processes involved, the ways in which the microphones were to be moved, the electronic circuits, the ways in which the players interact, were notated in the form of a set of instructions. In *Kurzwellen* (1968) the score indicates the ways in which the performers are to react both to the other performers, to what they have just played and to what is occurring on short-wave radios.

The extreme of non-involvement by the composer is found in the work written after a week of fasting and meditation in 1968, *Aus den Sieben Tagen*. In one of the sections of this, the musicians are instructed to play only when they have achieved a state of non-thinking, and to stop playing again when they begin to think.

It is an indication of the care with which Stockhausen prepared the scores and performances of his works that, in spite of their uncompromising modernity, new technical resources and constant exploration of the borders of music, they have a style which is recognizably his. This style is partly created by his fondness for certain instrumental and electronic sounds and textures. (The use of an amplified tam-tam is one recurring sonority.) Another distinctive texture/performance technique is the effect of one group of sounds interacting with (or 'modulating') another through the use of a ring modulator or other electronic device. This process, which is sometimes called intermodulation, was one of the ways in which a highly successful synthesis of natural and electronic sounds was achieved. In *Mikrophonie II*, microphones from a choir are fed into a ring modulator together with the output of a Hammond organ. The effect of a ring modulator is to produce new sounds which are a mixture of the pitches going into it, although the original sounds are lost, or audible in varying amounts with a greatly changed character. Smooth or startling transitions from natural to electronic sounds can be made, which Stockhausen does with great subtlety. The actual notes which the singers and organist produce are not all precisely notated since the process of modulation is the most important feature of the work. In another work, *Solo*, written in 1965–66, the electronics, consisting of a complex delay and feedback system, constitute almost the entire composition. The performer plays on any melody instrument. Four technical assistants · are required to manipulate microphone and playback levels, feedback, and to switch playback heads: it is mainly to them, not the performer, that the score is directed.

There is no doubt it is much easier to be aware of the relationships between the basic elements of a piece and the performers when a work like *Mikrophonie I* is performed: one can see the microphonists moving around the large gong while faders and knobs are manipulated.

(Top): **Karlheinz Stockhausen** and *(above)* **Kurzwellen**. This work is scored for piano tam-tam, viola, electronium and four short-wave radios played by the performers. The + signs indicate a rise in pitch, or increase in volume or duration of the note; the − signs the reverse. *(Right)*: **György Ligeti**

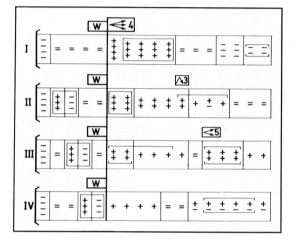

EUROPE AND AMERICA

Although Stockhausen has been discussed as probably the most interesting and representative figure in European electronic music, nearly all avant-garde musicians were at this point involved with comparable procedures in some way or other. Many other composers were working with electronics during the 1950s and 1960s, indeed few avant-garde composers did not. Belgian composer Henri Pousseur wrote one of the first pieces in Europe to use indeterminacy in *Scambi* (1957), which was also one of the first pieces to use noise as its sole material (i.e. electronically produced noise as opposed to the recorded noises of *musique concrète*). Pousseur also worked with tape in live performance in *Rimes pour différentes sources sonores*, written in 1958–59. Several other composers were beginning to combine taped music and instruments in performance, the first of whom was the Argentinian Mauricio Kagel, living in Cologne, in his *Transicion II* (1958–59). Both this and the Pousseur work were abstract instrumental pieces, using the tape recorder to transform instrumental timbres.

Mauricio Kagel pioneered the tape recorder as a performance instrument in his *Transicion II*

There were many possibilities for drama inherent in live electronic performance: the suggestions of space achieved by using several loudspeakers, the quick changes of dynamics, the use of speech as a basis for musical compositions, the element of surprise and shock, and the novelty of the equipment. Several composers wrote actual theatre pieces in the medium. Kagel's *Tremens* (1963–65) is a satirical one-act play with music and electronics in a hospital setting. The tape pieces of Italian Luigi Nono are both highly theatrical and fiercely political. *La Fabbrica illuminata* (1964) features a soprano (live or recorded) singing a protest against industrial labour to a concrete background of noises recorded in an Italian factory.

In America, where electronic music was developed with characteristic pioneering enthusiasm, there was considerable emphasis on live performance and 'mixed media' events. Studio music also flourished, although along rather different lines from those in Europe.

The first synthesizer – the RCA Mark One – was developed by 1955. The more sophisticated Mark Two version was set up at the Columbia Princeton Electronic music Center in 1959. The synthesizer, although not easy to use or to programme, was ideally suited to the production of serial compositions, since all the parameters – pitch, duration, timbre and dynamics – could be controlled with total accuracy. It was first used by Milton Babbitt, whose interest in serial composition paralleled that of the composers of the Cologne studio. Babbitt's works for synthesizer dating from the early 1960s, *Composition for Synthesizer* (1960–61) and *Ensembles for Synthesizer* (1962–64), are strictly composed, dense, polyphonic works which use the synthesizer as a kind of super-performance machine. *Philomel* (1963) is a more dramatic work, setting a live soprano against a prerecorded tape, also including a voice to express the metamorphosis of Philomel into a nightingale in Ovid's story.

Babbitt was joined at the Columbia Princeton Center by two of the other pioneers of tape music in America, Luening and Ussachevsky.

On the West Coast, Morton Subotnick was active in electronic music, although his most interesting activities came with the availability of synthesizers a few years later. In Canada, electronic activities centred around the studio established in Toronto and the work of Le Caine. However, the most interesting and original electronic activities in America were initiated by John Cage and his associates.

ELECTRONICS IN PERFORMANCE: CAGE

Cage is the most influential and challenging composer of the post-war period, and the most baffling. The first composer to use electronics as a basis for creating new music, he has continued to use them in most of his subsequent compositions.

Cage's pre-electronic works show a constant desire to extend the range of sounds from the instruments available, and a concern with sounds and textures not generally found in Western music. This is seen in the works for prepared piano with which he achieved some notoriety in the 1940s and 1950s. In these, a conventional piano is given a new range of sounds, mostly percussive, by the insertion of various objects on, and among, the strings. The influence of the Far East is seen both in the sounds, which have some affinity with the Balinese Gamelan (the percussion 'orchestra' which had fascinated Western composers since Debussy), and in the way in which the piano, the instrument most associated with individual

Composers from Debussy to Cage have been influenced by the timbres and rhythms of the **gamelan orchestra**

expression by nearly all the great composers since Mozart, is depersonalized into a percussion instrument, the group of instruments traditionally least associated with self-expression. The idea of loss of self in music was one that was to be an important key to the understanding of Cage's music of the next two decades.

Cage, like Varèse, whose music he admired, had sensed the potential for creating music with electronics before the technology was sufficiently developed. After such quasi-electronic experiments as the use of variable-speed gramophone turntables (playing test tones), it was to be expected that he should use true electronic resources as soon as they became available. Cage made probably the first use of amplification to create new sounds rather than merely to make something louder in *Imaginary Landscape No. 2* (1942), although in this work electronics played only a partial role. The first work entirely for electronic resources, *Imaginary Landscape No. 4* (1951), used twelve radios, each independently operated for volume and tuning by two performers.

In one sense this work could be seen as 'instant *musique concrète*', although it is doubtful if this is what Cage intended – at least in the generally accepted Schaefferian sense of organized sound with some kind of emotional overtone. Like the tape composition of a year later,

Williams Mix, and most of Cage's other works by this time, *Imaginary Landscape No. 4* was indeterminate in its composition, by the use of chance operations in deciding a rhythmic scheme. Since it could not be predicted what would be on the radio, it was also indeterminate in its execution.

The concept of indeterminacy, which in its simplest definition means a musical operation, the outcome of which is not known in advance, is central to an understanding of Cage's work and that of many of the subsequent electronic and experimental composers in America.

In America, unlike Europe, there was not the sense of needing to relate to a musical tradition going back centuries. The most 'American' composers had been individualists, musical pioneers like Ives, Cowell or Partch, working more or less alone; or composers in a popular tradition that had its roots in folk music, such as Foster, Joplin or Gershwin. Cage continued in this tradition of finding an individual solution to the problems of musical expression; European composers he admired tended to be the lesser-known heroes such as Satie and Varèse. It was in this untrammelled, intellectual atmosphere that Cage, finding that conventional methods of composition and performance with an emphasis on 'self-expression' through melody and harmony too restricting, applied Eastern aesthetic concepts to his work. He felt that there was a liberating effect in removing self, in the form of individual decisions, from some of the processes of music. One way in which this could be achieved was in the acceptance of chance as a part of composition or performance. Chance operations with electronic devices tend to be especially interesting, since the effect of a small movement or sound, which might otherwise be insignificant, can be magnified to epic strength. Coinciding as it did with the increasing use of indeterminacy in his works, electronics strengthened and extended the concept. Although used in varying forms by many other composers, including those in Europe after the late 1950s, no other composer applied chance to music as rigorously as Cage.

In *Imaginary Landscape No. 4*, the composer's role consisted of setting up a situation in which radio broadcasts can be heard not for their content but for their sound, as part of a musical performance. There is also a surreal element in the unusual combinations of information that may occur, a parody of a familiar contemporary situation. Although indeterminate, it avoids any element of improvisation.

THE REVOLUTION IN NOTATION

Cage's electronic works divide into those which are notated, usually by chance methods, and those consisting of a performance in which various events are allowed to occur. Many combine the two. The *Imaginary Landscape* series and *Variations I-VIII* explore various aspects of musical performance with little intervention on the composer's part. Particularly in the case of the *Variations* this is achieved with the use of graphic 'scores' which are so different from the conventional idea of a musical score that they need some explanation.

Most of the earliest electronic music, being composed on tape, required no score. When live electronic music began, it was realized that most traditional forms of notation were inadequate because there was no provision for notating noise, except as percussion, or for notating timbre, except as combinations of conventional instruments. Both of these were major elements of electronic composition. The notation was also superfluous because in a very large number of works, both in Europe and America, precise notation of the traditional values of pitch, rhythm and dynamics was either of no real importance or secondary to the effects of electronic processes or individual reactions to other sonic events. Although scores were not necessary for tape compositions realized in the studio, in the traditional sense of a score conveying the composer's intentions to performers, composers often published a score of some kind, either for study and explanation, as a visual reference in possible performance with live instruments or for copyright purposes. In addition a few composers, notably Stockhausen, prepared scores for the relatively rare situation of someone wishing to realize another version of a studio piece. Even with scores as precise as Stockhausen's for the *Studies I & II*, which notate the relative levels and pitches of sine wave generators and the envelope of notes pseudo-scientifically, this is something almost impossible to do accurately. One suspects that the main motive was the personal satisfaction of the composer in showing how thoroughly he had approached the composition, and in preparing a handsome piece of graphics.

By the time live electronic music had become more common than studio composition, requiring at the very least some technical explanation,

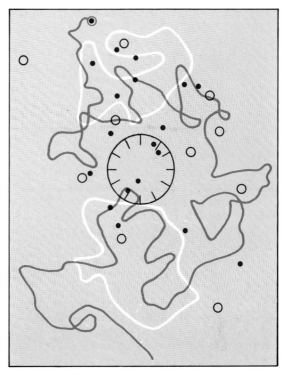

John Cage has pursued several different paths in his attempts to find a truly random method of composition, including casting lots according to the **I Ching** *(left)* or the elaborate permutations of **Cartridge Music** *(above)*

a kind of tradition had been established in the preparation of scores which, by using a variety of graphic and musical notations, were by turn instructional, philosophical, witty, whimsical, poetic or merely decorative. There seems to have been an acceptance of the fact that it was almost impossible to convey all the information necessary regarding even relatively simple electronic set-ups and their use to performers who did not have some prior knowledge of them. Two other factors were also important in reducing the necessity for exact notation. One was the widespread dissemination of music through recordings and broadcasts. The other was that most composers were also performers and supervised rehearsal of their works just as composers of an earlier era had done.

In the case of Cage's compositions, since the composer did not wish to control the actual notes which were performed, the poetic, philosophical and visual aspects of the scores assumed great importance. With wide-ranging interests and abilities in literature and art, and with a background of experiment in notation going back to before the electronic period, his scores are some of the finest examples of a new relationship between composer and performer.

Cage's scores vary in their degree of purely musical information as opposed to other aspects of performance. At one extreme is *4′33″* (1952), which requires a performer simply to sit at a piano for that length of time and not play. This takes a belief in the aesthetic value of chance, and therefore an acceptance of any sounds that might occur, together with an implied assumption that the only absolute values in music are sound and silence, to a logical conclusion. It also expresses in simple form the belief that the only requirement for a musical performance is that there is an audience, since sounds are occurring continuously. (Cage's discovery in the totally echoless, soundproof room called an anechoic chamber that there is no such thing as silence, is something to which he has frequently referred in his writings.)

More typical of Cage's compositions is *Cartridge Music*, dating from 1960. Earlier electronic works such as *Imaginary Landscapes 1—4* and *Credo In Us* (1942) has used a notated rhythmic structure, prepared in advance by tossing coins (using the ancient Chinese oracle method, the I-Ching); in the case of the latter work a pattern was worked out to indicate raising and lowering of a gramophone needle on to a record of an orchestral 'classic' while piano and percussion play other rhythmic parts. However, by the time of *Cartridge Music*, even this degree of structure had been abandoned.

The piece is for performers on gramophone cartridges, into which instead of needles an object such as a toothpick or pipe cleaner has been inserted. The cartridge then becomes a highly sensitive microphone, amplifying whatever it touches, in the same way as it would a record. The score consists of twenty sheets of blob-like shapes, a sheet of instructions and four transparent sheets, one of which has a circle marked like a stop watch, one with dots, one with circles and one with a dotted line. With these materials 'each performer makes his own part', by placing the sheets on top of each other and performing in certain ways according to the intersections of the various shapes: dots, circles and lines. For example, intersection of the dotted line with a point within a shape indicates that a sound is produced in any manner on the object inserted in the cartridge (each cartridge being represented by a shape). The composer does not specify what sounds are to be made, although the specification of the technology involved ensures that they will mostly consist of noise. The composer points out that all events ordinarily thought to be undesirable are to be accepted in this situation. 'One may take that as a boast or a warning', commented the English critic Paul Griffiths.

It is a problem for the listener with many of Cage's works that they are often unpleasant to listen to and extremely boring. Cage is well aware of this, taking the moralistic line that such an ordeal was good for the perceptions generally. An overreliance on smug Zen Buddhist answers to criticism of this philosophy now makes some of the more polemical writings and compositions of the sixties seem a little hollow. Nevertheless Cage is that rare figure, the truly experimental composer. Virtually no aspect of electronic music was not anticipated or invented by him. *Cartridge Music*, coming four years before Stockhausen's *Mikrophonie I*, undoubtedly had a great influence on live electronic music. Also, although the point can be overstressed, Cage's visits to Europe in the 1950s contributed to the breakdown of the rigid ideas of serialism and to the use (at first cautiously) of indeterminacy there.

IMAGES OF NATURE

If serialism could be seen as an extreme form of classicism, with antecedents in renaissance and baroque counterpoint, then indeterminacy is the extreme of romanticism. The overwhelming quality of Cage's works is love of nature, a love more closely observed and more impressive than that of Beethoven or Wordsworth, in that it is totally without sentiment. Cage seeks to imitate nature not in appearance or even in the use of 'natural' sounds, but 'in her manner of operation'. This has allowed the remarkable achievement of an appreciation of the natural world which is as appropriate in Manhattan as it is in the English Lake District. There may appear to be an absolution of all responsibility for a composition in this.

But what Cage has retained, against all that he has relinquished, is the responsibility for the structure in which events happen. *Variations IV* is one of the most indeterminate of the series of variations. The score consists of a transparent sheet of dots to be dropped on to a map or plan of the performance area. Sound-generating activity is to take place on lines drawn as a result of these activities where they go outside the theatre space. Yet these sounds are as firmly fixed within the composition as the clouds in a Constable landscape are fixed within their frame, although their shape, if true to nature, was likewise created indeterminately.

It is perhaps one of the most attractive features of modernism in the arts that, as in a good thriller, the audience is deliberately shocked and confused, only to discover at the end that everything is left much the same as it was at the beginning. The works of the Impressionists, who were once thought to be so relentlessly modern as to be destroying art, now hang in countless living-rooms. The composers of the post-war avant-garde have all been trying in different ways to create images of nature or of the universe, which relates to a technological world. They have approached this from several different directions. Stockhausen and the serial composers, by extending what they saw as an essential underlying structure, found that the sounds ultimately produced were virtually indistinguishable from those produced by chance methods. Further liberation from the intellectual restrictions of European tradition was achieved in Stockhausen's case by exposure to Eastern thought (which had already had such a profound effect on Cage).

The sounds of nature, in Cage's view, are not confined to the countryside; the everyday noises of city life are equally valid

The music of **Morton Feldman** seems static, but for him, sound quality is the criterion

MUSIC AND MOVEMENT

Electronics is uniquely suited to the kind of indeterminate process in which a circuit produces a particular kind of result, although the details vary. (An obvious analogy is with an acorn, which always produces a recognizable oak tree, although the branches are always arranged differently.) Cage and his associates, particularly the pianist David Tudor and composer Gordon Mumma, became highly involved in producing new specialized electronic circuits as the technology became available, usually in connection with some sort of theatrical or visual event.

Cage's interest in theatre goes back many years. His 1952 composition *Water Music*, although not particularly electronic in character, used a large poster-size score, placing the conductor in the role of conjuror, and adding a strong visual element. Cage's philosophy, implied in many of his compositions (especially those from the sixties on), that the major requirement for a musical performance was an audience, presupposed a degree of theatre, since it was clearly important that people should be aware that a performance was taking place. He collaborated in another theatre event, with Merce Cunningham, at Black Mountain College, N.C., using various mixed media; in what is generally considered the first 'happening'. The Cunningham Co. was formed in 1952 with Cage as Musical Director, and artist Robert Rauschenberg as designer. However, following the strong belief in the value of chance, events were generally intended to take place simultaneously but independently. There was no connection with the traditional relationship of music, dance and design in emphasizing drama or conveying narrative. In *Variations V* (1965), for example, the dancers are partly responsible for the sounds which accompany them, by the use of antennae on stage which sense their movements, although in ways which create a sense of opposition rather than co-operation. This self-conscious avoidance of a relationship leads instead to what seems like deliberate obscurity. Cage's works involving speech (another field in which his work was startlingly innovative) often use the reference point of intelligibility and non-intelligibility to emphasize speech as sound rather than meaning. This is another aesthetic use of deliberate confusion. The delivery of a long 'lecture' in which only the first few sentences are heard as speech is the

Xenakis, by the use of mathematics (and sometimes aided by the most potent tool of the late twentieth century, the digital computer), evolved another view of music which treats sound as analogous to all the other movements of large numbers of individual particles underlying the structure of matter. By applying the law of large numbers evolved in the eighteenth century, known as stochastic theory, which states that the more often an indeterminate action is repeated (such as tossing a coin), the more it will tend towards a determinate end, Xenakis developed a method of composition which enabled him to express in music his sense of the unity of nature.

One of the closest associates of Cage in the fifties was the composer Morton Feldman, whose compositions, which often included the use of electronic generators and other devices, have an organic quality in that the composer only specifies the general areas in which the musicians play. In some works rhythms were specified but pitches only suggested (*Projections*, 1950–51); in others, pitch but not duration (*The Swallows of Salangan*, 1960). The effect is almost static, a slowly shifting musical landscape – which is a description the composer would probably endorse.

same kind of forced education in the value of sounds as instrumental compositions which feature substantial chunks of unpleasant noise. The electronic distortion of speech was presaged by the sequence of stories which make up *Indeterminacy* (1958), each being delivered in one minute, irrespective of length. This led to some stories being spoken very quickly, others very slowly, running counter to all accepted ideas of narration. The delivery was accompanied by taped or live electronic music. It is a reflection on Cage's success as a seer and teacher that very few have tried to imitate his work directly, although many have been influenced by it to varying degrees. It is an interesting observation on electronic and experimental music since the 1960s that the one consistent influence has been a composer whose own work is unified solely by its use of chance and open-mindedness in the search for new sounds and techniques.

From the mid-sixties on it is fair to say that there were almost as many approaches to electronic composition as there were composers.

A cartoon of 1911 depicts an uncannily accurate portrayal of a multi-media presentation in this jibe at the music of the future. *(Below):* **John Cage's** *Variations V* (1965) in which the proximity of the dancers to the thin rods affects the resulting sound

The most dramatic technical development of the period, the voltage-controlled synthesizer, had a surprisingly small impact on serious electronic music, although its effect on popular music was more obvious.

Leaving aside the RCA synthesizer, which had been developed largely as a scientific and technical exercise to which relatively few musicians had access, synthesizers in the general sense of the word were developed with the close co-operation of musicians. The first two voltage-controlled synthesizers were the Synket, developed in Rome in 1965 by Paul Ketoff for use by the composer John Eaton, and the much better-known Moog, first used in the same year by composer Max Deutsch. In California, Subotnick worked closely with engineer and inventor Donald Buchla in the development of the synthesizer that bears his name. The Buchla, unlike the other main synthesizers of the sixties, did not feature a keyboard. This made it generally unsuitable for the roles in which the Moog became most familiar: popular re-creations of the classics and, later, in rock music. All synthesizers, however, had a tendency to lead composers towards the use of sounds with a certain inherent attractiveness, seen in such early synthesizer works as Subotnick's *Silver Apples of the Moon* (1967). This contrasted with the often harsh sounds used in earlier electronic music derived from amplified natural sounds, and led to some increased public acceptance of electronic music.

Although synthesizers were used in live performance, particularly the inexpensive models such as the Putney, and in the realization of some computer-controlled music, in general composers eschewed the predictability of such factory devices.

The use of technology and sound-systems becomes very important in much of the music of the mid-sixties and the seventies, reflecting both the scientific optimism of the era of manned space flight and cynicism with regard to the faith placed in the mass media. Art reflected a culture increasingly obsessed with science by creating pseudo-science, a process begun in the visual arts long before by Marcel Duchamp.

David Tudor's *Rainforest* (1968) echoed the growing interest in ecology by creating musical devices which 'recycle' sounds. As in many of Tudor's compositions, the technology necessary for performance was specially made. In this case it consisted of 'instrumental loudspeakers', transducers attached to resonators of varying substances which reproduced the sounds of oscillators played through them with differing resonance. By relaying the output from these instrumental loudspeakers to conventional loudspeakers, a feedback system was established making the whole (in Mumma's words) an ecologically balanced sound system.

Because the establishment of the sound system was in many cases the final act of the composer – in the works of Tudor, Mumma and his colleagues of the Sonic Arts Union (Behrman, Lucier, Ashley and Neuhaus) – there is little comment to be made beyond a description of the set-ups, except to mention again the way in which music was frequently seen as a continuous process analogous to sculpture or architecture, a part of the environment. Works were often created with the idea of continuous performance, usually in collaboration with artists from different disciplines (including film and video). Cage has quoted Erik Satie, one of the co-opted heroes of the American avant-garde, as saying 'we must bring about a music which is like furniture – a music, that is, which will be part of the noises of the environment, will take them into consideration'. Many composers took this suggestion to heart, or independently arrived at the same conclusion. In some cases they were responding to the increasing levels of sound in society, both in the commercial environmental sounds of Muzak, and in the noise of everything from aircraft to televisions.

LaMonte Young has extended environmental compositions to extraordinary lengths, a week or more in performance, electronic devices playing an essential part. An early influence was the sound of wind coming through the chinks in the log cabin where he was born, or so it is often reported, with an acceptance of American mythology which is surprising in its lack of cynicism. After early serial compositions, Young developed his own theories of composition, influenced to some extent by Cage, through long, almost static harmonies to a form of indeterminacy, where the title of the score may constitute the composition. This can be whimsical and poetic, as in *Some of them were very old Grasshoppers*. In others long titles seem to have become merely pedantic, some of the sections of the work composed 'continuously' during the 1960s, *The Tortoise, his Dreams and Journeys*, paralleling the length in performance with abundant verbiage.

The ideas of length in performance played an important part in quite different types of electronic music of the sixties. Long improvisatory performances of a specified work, or untitled improvisations, were given by several groups established for that purpose.

Electronic music improvisation developed from several sources. On the one hand there was the influence of Cage, although it should be pointed out that he did not in general advocate improvisation in the conventional sense of individual self-expression, indicating rather an impersonal acceptance of whatever sound events occurred. On the other hand there was some influence of jazz, in which self-expression is paramount. In the London-based Improvisation group AMM, which included composer Cornelius Cardew (at one time considerably influenced by Cage) and several jazz musicians, indeterminacy and self-expression both seemed to be secondary to social and to some extent political considerations. Co-operation among musicians was sometimes seen as comparable to the idealized view of the association of industrial workers, which underlay the more romantic kinds of socialism fashionable in the sixties.

Live performance ensembles were formed in most countries where there was an awareness of electronic music. The first in Europe was the Gruppo di Improvvisazione Nuove Consonanza, formed in Rome in 1964, and followed two years later by another Rome-based group, Musica Elettronica Viva. Both groups contained a large proportion of Americans. Although at first there was some performance of composed music, the emphasis became improvisatory, including the concept of the 'sound pool', a concert environment involving large-scale audience participation. It tended towards fairly general electronic technology rather than the complex and specialized circuits that were developed for some live performances in America, such as those which centred around the ONCE group. This latter was a development from the ONCE festivals which took place in Ann Arbor, Michigan, from 1960 to 1967: multimedia events which involved electronic music among many other visual and theatrical resources. An offshoot of the ONCE groups was the Sonic Arts Union, formed in 1966, the members of which have already been mentioned as being major developers of new electronic music performance technology during the late 1960s and early 1970s.

In Europe the other main activities in live electronic music took place in Germany and England. In Germany, Stockhausen's influence was very strong, both in his own group and in others such as Feedback (which included some

of his former associates).

The direction taken in live electronic and experimental performance groups in England can be taken as symptomatic of a general trend in attitudes towards electronic music which became noticeable in nearly all countries by the 1970s. Initially concerned with the use of conventional instruments and relatively low-tech electronic devices, groups such as The Gentle Fire and Naked Software, as well as AMM, pursued the approach sometimes called electro-acoustic. But in several cases the acoustic began to become more prominent. AMM gave way to a much looser association of players which made up the Scratch Orchestra, a collaboration of a large number of occasional players using a wide range of instruments, with no particular emphasis on electronics (although some players and groups such as Intermodulation continued to use electronics extensively). Later English ensembles of the avant-garde, the Portsmouth Sinfonia, for example, which featured performance of such classical favourites as the *William Tell* overture and Beethoven's Fifth Symphony performed by people unable to play their instruments, were almost entirely acoustic in their line-up.

Various leading composers who had once been enthusiastically involved with electronic music, such as Xenakis and Berio, have tended since the late 1960s to use more conventional instrumentation, although electronics are used here and there without ceremony as part of the resources available to all contemporary composers. (It is also probable that many of the textures and compositional techniques of these and other composers would not have evolved without electronic music: for example, Berio's use of speech, or Xenakis's dense orchestral writing.)

In America, a trend away from involvement with electronics can also be detected. A style of composition and performance relying heavily on tape loops, other feedback systems and repeated ostinatos became apparent in the mid-sixties. The main protagonists were Terry Riley and Steve Reich (also LaMonte Young), and the style is sometimes referred to as minimalist. The main stylistic feature is the creation of slowly shifting patterns and complex internal rhythms out of simple melodic and rhythmic cells. It was considered important that the relationship of small parts to the whole could be clearly heard, and that there was a certain hypnotic effect often deriving from the overall length and slow development. Riley's

Seen here with **Brian Eno**, Salvador Dali ('The cultural centre of the world is the railway buffet at Perpignan') is a professed admirer of the work of Roxy Music

Steve Reich *(below)* has exploited the effects of phasing music in time both acoustically and electronically

1964 composition *In C* is considered a classic of the genre. Most of the earlier pieces were created with tape or other electronic resources. However, the trend in both composers' works, particularly that of Reich, and of the English minimalist composers whose works have been recorded on the *Obscure* label under the direction of Brian Eno, is towards the increasing use of acoustic instruments. Sometimes the use of the recording studio has replaced the tape recorders that would have been used in live performance. But the general trend is clear: complex electronic circuits no longer have the almost magical appeal they once had. Perhaps Neil Armstrong's boot burst that particular bubble, and music has begun to reflect the preoccupations of a world more worried about the increasing sophistication of weapons, the integrity of governments which use electronic technology for bugging rather than the old belief in science as synonymous with progress.

However, there were fields of music where new electronic technology was being used with all the enthusiasm of kids with new toys (often with the same finesse): the mass media, films, television and rock.

THE BUSINESS

Although the activities of the serious avant-garde have produced most of what is generally thought of as electronic music, other applications of electronics to music more popular and accessible have had a far more profound influence. This is the more so because the role of electronics is so familiar and universal that it is often not noticed at all.

There are two main ways in which electronics dominate musical life in the Western World: as an essential part of the creation and performance of popular music and as an essential part of the technology of recording and broadcasting by which virtually all music, past and present, is universally disseminated. In this respect musical life in the Third World is equally affected, perhaps even more so through the domination of the air waves by music of a different culture.

Because of the development of the mass communication media – records, radio, films and television – popular music has had an impact far exceeding that of any popular music of the pre-electronic age. Of these, film was the first to use electronics in a creative way. Indeed much of the early uses of film sound rep-

resented the most imaginative uses to which electronics had been put. Some of this was in connection with experimental film, which was clearly closer to art music than to pop, for example the early experiments of Moholy-Nagy or of Avraamov in Russia. However, composers of music for films intended for a mass audience were quick to realize the ways in which dramatic effects could be heightened by the use of the technology.

Prokofiev, one of the greatest composers to have written for film, can also be considered the first record producer in that he preferred to be in the control booth during film recording sessions of his music rather than on the rostrum, so that he could hear what was actually going to be heard by the audience. He (and the Russian sound engineers) soon realized the dramatic possibilities of changing the natural balance of instruments by the way in which microphones were placed. One of the earliest examples of a deliberate electronic effect must be the deliberate distortion of the trumpets in the music for *Alexander Nevsky* (recorded in 1938) by placing the microphone very close to the instruments.

The experiments of the Whitney brothers with electronically created music made directly on to film, to accompany abstract animation, comes in an area between experimental music

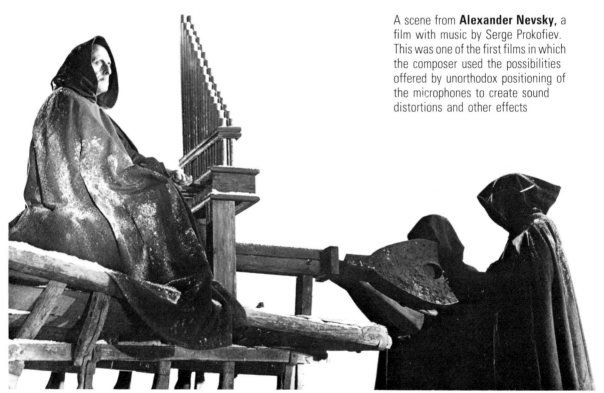

A scene from **Alexander Nevsky,** a film with music by Serge Prokofiev. This was one of the first films in which the composer used the possibilities offered by unorthodox positioning of the microphones to create sound distortions and other effects

and a desire to create a reasonably popular art form. Cage admired their work in the thirties as being ahead of its time, and the public accepted electronic sounds more readily when they were linked with something visual. (A kind of accompaniment to this theme is provided by Walt Disney's abstract animations that go with Bach's Toccata and Fugue in D minor in *Fantasia*.) The work of the Canadian Norman McLaren comes in the same category, his abstract sound animation being so widely shown as not to be really considered experimental.

The use of electronic instruments in science fiction films rapidly became something of a cliché, and extends from the thirties to the present day in films, radio and television. The way in which most people hear almost any piece of electronic music has been indelibly coloured by the spine-chilling wail of a theremin in *They Came from Outer Space*, or the roar of the monsters from the id in *Forbidden Planet*. No one would claim any great artistic achievements in these exercises, and even those who admire the genre would have to admit that the advantage of familiarization of the public with electronic timbres is probably outweighed by the over-strong association of sine waves with monsters. Nevertheless electronics were most effectively used in some non-sci-fi films, such as Miklos Rozsa's score for *Lost Weekend*, in which the sound of the theremin is used to parallel the confusion and disintegration of the alcoholic mind. Many other electronic techniques were pioneered by film composers, who were able to use effects that would have been considered too radical if they had not been used in a dramatic context, in much the same way as atonality and dissonance began to be used by such composers as Bernard Herrmann without the public being aware of anything beyond their own involvement with the dramatic situation.

Popular music slipped into reliance on electronic resources during the 1930s and 1940s via the importance of income from record sales and radio, and by the electrification of instruments (primarily in order to increase their volume). By the time rock and roll was recognized as an entirely new phenomenon of popular music, the electrification was almost complete. Here was a musical style which owed both its sound and its dissemination to electronics. In a uniquely twentieth-century process, each succeeding stylistic development, as well as each boost to the music's phenomenal popularity, increased the reliance on technology.

It is a common mistake to see as 'electronic'

only that small area of pop music which self-consciously imitates, or is comparable with, the use of electronics by the serious avant-garde. This view fails to grasp either the ways in which pop music is self-styled or the innocence of its eclecticism.

The development of the most essential sound of rock, the electric guitar, is a good example of the way in which developments in rock music are an inseparable mixture of various technological developments, individual invention and experiment, and market forces. The electric guitar had first been developed in the twenties and thirties by several different inventors and musicians working independently. The first successful commercial instruments were Hawaiian and steel guitars for country music, since they were the instruments most in need of amplification. During the 1940s further developments were made, producing several of the guitars most widely used in rock, such as

the Telecaster and the Les Paul, although their inventors could not have in any way anticipated the kind of sounds, now so familiar, which have since been produced from them.

The classic sound of the electric guitar only became possible with the use of amplification developed much later. Country music, which is what most electric guitar manufacturers had in mind when they produced their earlier models, is a vocally dominated style with a tradition of folksy (but virtuoso) acoustic instrumental playing. Rock and roll, even when it first appeared, emphasized the rhythm section much more than its ancestors – blues or country music – had done, and added the essentially modern and urban values of volume and aggressive energy, with a consequent reliance on modern technology. (It was also specifically designed to be heard on the radio and juke box.) Since rock musicians have tended to be improvisers rather than innovators, they have

Daphne Oram, in the **BBC Radiophonic Workshop**. A pioneer in the introduction of electronic music methods into schools, she is seen here demonstrating a tape loop technique

In Miklos Rozsa's score for the film *The Lost Weekend*, the Hungarian-born composer used the disturbing tones of the theremin to accompany the onset of alcoholic hallucinations

(Right): **Mark Knopfler** of Dire Straits and his steel guitar

(Far right): In the early days of rock and roll, before it was commonplace for a teenager to own a record player, the **juke-box** was the usual outlet for the latest pop music

adapted existing instruments to the requirements of their style rather than created new ones. Since, too, they have been part of a highly successful industry, manufacturers have provided a steady stream of new technological developments with which to work.

There is another consideration, however, that of originality. Rock audiences have constantly craved the new and exciting. In order to remain competitive, rock musicians have had to use the resources placed at their disposal in ways which are always exciting and original, while remaining more or less within the limited musical conventions of the genre. It is this which has given rock music its energy and power. When 1940s guitar design was combined with the power of the late 1960s amplification and the creative imagination and theatrical flair of a musician such as Hendrix or Clapton, the result could be both genuinely original and modern, yet at the same time part of a tradition, something only rarely achieved by the electronic avant-garde.

Of course groups and individuals working within the rock tradition have sometimes produced genuinely original ideas, technical and musical, although the vast majority of new concepts in electronic music were inventions of the avant-garde. The major breakthroughs in the uses of electronic resources made by rock musicians have come in the areas of live performance: in the use of amplification, distortion and effects pedals, or in the recording studio.

As soon as it was realized that the recording studio could be used for more than the simple taping of a live performance, which happened in the early days of rock and roll, possibilities for the creation of new and more ambitious sounds were quick to be exploited. The addition of reverb and echo – mainly to voices though sometimes to other instruments – produced a new concept in the use of the voice as something partly human, partly mechanical. The use of classic rock and roll repeat echo is heard on many records such as Elvis Presley's 'Heartbreak Hotel' or Gene Vincent's 'Be Bop-A-Lula'.

The use of the studio, initially for such effects as these but later in much more ambitious ways, also changed the role of the producer from someone who merely commented on musical performance to that of a new kind of artist whose ideas could have as much influence on the final record as those of the performers.

In the case of the first great producer in pop,

Phil Spector, the musicians appeared subservient, manipulated by the Svengali-like figure of the producer. Spector used a large number of musicians, all playing much the same part. The musicians were deliberately tired out by long sessions and repetitive parts, in order to produce an impersonal element in the wall of sound, the phrase most often used to describe the echo-laden, quasi-orchestral texture of Spector's records. Spector's great achievement was the way in which he showed that a record need not sound in any way like a live performance, indeed that commercial success could be greater if the studio's potential for new sounds could be exploited. He also showed that extensive use of electronic effects, far from standardizing the sound, could make it intensely personal. Rock music thus became the first major musical style, apart from the music produced at the same time by the serious avant-garde, which was not related primarily to live performance.

The eclecticism which became a distinctive feature of rock music in the sixties included some influences from avant-garde music, together with the inclusion of ideas from Western classical music or Eastern instruments. The use of cut-up tape reassembled at random on

(Above): **Ravi Shankar,** the celebrated exponent of the music of India, has had a far-reaching influence on musicians of the twentieth century.
(Right): **John Cale,** one of the Velvet Underground

the *Sergeant Pepper* album is an example. Another is the use of drones and ostinato patterns in 'Tomorrow Never Knows' (from *Revolver*). The influence of Eastern music as well as electronics on this track is symptomatic of its effects upon much avant-garde music, particularly in the 'minimalist' school, probably the area of serious music to have most affinity with rock. Several direct collaborations, such as that between Terry Riley and John Cale, have been moderately successful.

The fact that the rock audience, exposed to music of increasing complexity and originality throughout the sixties, from such bands as The Mothers of Invention and the Grateful Dead, the Velvet Underground or the Pink Floyd were receptive to some of the music of the avant-garde may have encouraged serious composers to expand their audience, particularly by presenting new music in a more theatrical, less 'concert hall' manner. Some musicians who had worked within the avant-garde realized that even a minority rock audience was larger than the existing serious audience, and transferred some of their activities accordingly. As well as Cale and others in America, several German groups of the late 1960s included members who had worked in serious electronic music, notably Can and Tangerine Dream.

By the start of the seventies, as the excesses of psychedelia gave way in one direction to a simpler rock and roll (such groups as Creedence Clearwater Revival or the Alman Brothers), other musicians – aware of the ability of rock to absorb and modify other musical traditions – were planning a new, more electronic direction. One important factor was the rapid expansion in the use of the newer electronic instruments such as synthesizers. (Another was the financial viability of even non-hit albums in a period of booming record sales.)

Rock musicians had always been enthusiastic users of synthesizers, in general more so than avant-garde musicians. By the early seventies, an enormous range of instruments was available. More than any other keyboard instrument, the synthesizer encouraged the flashy keyboard virtuosos, like Keith Emerson and Rick Wakeman. In another direction, jazz and funk players developed a use of the synthesizer that was closer to the human voice, by using its ability to bend notes and perform portamentos.

Many groups developed a consciously 'electronic' sound, using as many new instruments as possible and often treating the voice as well. Electronic sounds had become synonymous

(Right): **The Beach Boys.** Electronic sounds feature prominently in their record Good Vibrations, generally acclaimed to be one of the finest pop singles of all time

(Far right): **Kraftwerk** ('power station') a German group whose music is strongly influenced by their heavy industry background

Keith Emerson *(below)*, seen here at the synthesizer. His virtuosity on all manner of keyboard instruments, notably the electronic organ, has been accompanied by exhilarating and spectacular feats of showmanship

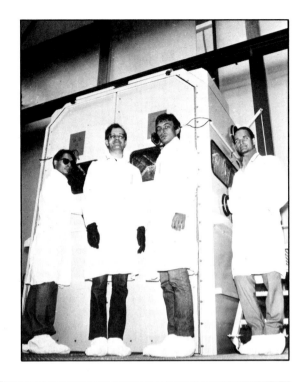

with contemporary life. Sometimes this was conscious, as in some of Bowie's albums from the mid-seventies or those of the German group Kraftwerk. Many of the 'new wave' groups of the late seventies have carried on this trend, in a self-conscious and pretentious use of technology.

Having no intellectual pretensions whatever, disco music, the main dance music of the last decade, relied equally on the use of electronics. The steady insistent rhythms were often obtained with the use of a rhythm box: careful use of the studio, as well as extensive use of synthesizers, ensured that this form of escapism (like the science fiction also in vogue) maintained the old optimism for the future.

As in the past, most of the best rock music remained a hybrid, although enriched by the availability of so many new instruments. It may be that the synthesizer and other new forms of instruments will be used in ways as hard to predict now as the guitar styles of the 1960s were impossible to foresee two decades before.

One of the major advantages of new electronic technology has been the increased sophistication of live performances, often with lights and theatrical effects of stunning complexity.

Rock and roll, however, although it has developed traditions of brilliant performance which complement (and in many cases extend) recorded versions, is nevertheless rooted in the recording studio and nurtured by radio. A rock artist is still only considered to have 'arrived' when he has at the very least a recording contract, if not a hit record. The audience is aware that records are no substitute for live performance, but rather a kind of idealized performance, produced from the air at will by the turn of a dial. There is no real element of substitution, since the sounds are created in exactly the same way for the audience as they were for the performers: through the activation of a loudspeaker by electrical impulses.

However, when the same situation occurs with orchestral music from the classical tradition, a very different set of aesthetic values is brought into play. When a piece of music is broadcast and simultaneously reproduced in a million loudspeakers, each one different, many of them in situations too bizarre to have been conceived by anyone not of the modern era, it becomes electronic music. It may be this fact, so familiar as to pass unnoticed, that has had the most profound effect on musical thinking in the twentieth century.

Luciano Berio's use of *musique concrète*, and blocks of sound moving physically from one loudspeaker to another, can be attributed to Stockhausen's influence, especially the latter's 'Gesang der' drei heilige Jünglinge'

B

MILTON BABBITT (1916...)

American composer and mathematician. Babbitt is one of the most significant figures in American music. His work is unequivocally serial, some of it taking the theories behind serial composition beyond pitch, to encompass timbres, note values and dynamic levels. This method is known as total serialism.

Babbitt began his music studies at the age of four, learning violin and clarinet; but his father soon infected the boy with his own fascination for mathematics. After graduating, he worked as a music critic while at the same time having lessons from the composer Roger Sessions. Later he joined the staff of Princeton University, teaching mathematics there during the war.

After the war, Babbitt actively championed serial composition by publishing various papers on the subject, and was invited to lecture on seminars and courses in Salzburg, Darmstadt and Berkshire (USA). His interest in electronic music dates from the early 1950s. With the aid of a Rockefeller Foundation grant, he was instrumental in setting up the Columbia-Princeton Electronic Music Center, established in 1959. From 1961 he wrote several works for the medium, including *Composition for Synthesizer* (composed for the RCA synthesizer), followed by *Vision and Prayer* to words by Dylan Thomas, the first work to be written for live performer and synthesizer. His best-known work may be *Philomel* (1963–64), for soprano and tape. In this piece the soprano line has a distinct classical form, with sections corresponding to recitative, arioso and aria.

LUCIANO BERIO (1925...)

Italian composer. Berio first studied music with his father, an organist and

composer. He studied in Milan and later at Tanglewood, where he had lessons in composition from Dallapiccola. From 1958 he worked for a while at Darmstadt, then moved to the USA in 1962, becoming a teacher of composition at the Juilliard School of Music. He married the soprano and composer Cathy Berberian, for whom he wrote several compositions. One of these, *Omaggio a Joyce* (1958), has as its starting point a recitation of passages from Joyce's *Ulysses*, which was then recorded and electronically transmuted.

Like many composers of electronic music, Berio soon concluded that no matter how ingenious the composition, music needs live participation. He has absorbed many twentieth-century techniques including serialism and aleatory methods, and often takes an earlier work (either his own, or a 'standard classic') and modifies it in a process of continual creation. His *Cela*

veut dire que . . . (1969–70), for example, uses a live chorus and pre-recorded utterances of phonemes, which are linked with the live sections by the interval of a tritone. Later, this work was expanded into a multi-media presentation with orchestral instruments, choreography and lighting effects added.

PIERRE BOULEZ (1925...)

French composer and conductor. In recent years Boulez has turned from composition to conducting, gaining a formidable reputation for his aural precision and accurate technique. Before 1960, however, he was considered by some to be a likely successor to Stravinsky. He studied composition with Messiaen, and later (after the liberation of France) serial techniques, proscribed by the Nazi régime, with René Leibowitz.

Boulez first came into prominence

In the title role of the film *The Man Who Fell to Earth*, **David Bowie** reversed his usual space-age image and portrayed an alien who takes on an earthmanlike appearance

After **Boulez** had started his experiments in electronic music, he withdrew an acoustic work because it was impossible to make the precise dynamics sufficiently evident

through his appearances at Darmstadt and Donaueschingen. His early works were in strict serial technique; and from Messiaen's *Mode de valeurs et d'intensités* he drew the concept that serialism need not be confined to pitch alone, but could be extended to dynamics and timbres. From 1950 he experimented with electronic music at the studio of Henry and Schaeffer, and in 1958 constructed his massive *Poésie pour pouvoir*. In this piece, transmuted recordings of Michaux's poetry are played through a vast array of loud-speakers that cause the sound to swirl around the auditorium, accompanied by a complex orchestral ensemble. Boulez now feels, however, that the effects he had visualized were not then technically capable of realization.

DAVID BOWIE (1947...)

English composer, producer, singer, guitarist and actor. Bowie's wilfully

bizarre personality has too often overshadowed his restless talent. His early desire for 'something fuller than music' led him to study art and mime as well. An early record, a squeaky novelty called 'The Laughing Gnome', was a gauche experiment in electronic effects. After a brief flirtation with psychedelia, he had a major hit single with 'Space Oddity' in 1969. He publicly flaunted his eccentricities, claiming bisexuality and appearing in a photograph that showed his wife and small child (Zowie Bowie), with himself in a full-length dress.

In 1972 he became a superstar and cult object with *The Rise and Fall of Ziggy Stardust and the Spiders from Mars*. Bowie, in orange hair, sequins and high boots, was Ziggy incarnate. Each successive album was presented on stage in shows that were as much theatre as they were music. His interest in working with different musical styles resulted in a brilliant but bewildering succession of albums during the mid-seventies. *Young Americans* (1975) and *Station to Station* (1976) anticipated the disco and soul revival which followed a few years later. But in his next two albums, *Low* and *Heroes*, the approach was deliberately – almost perversely – enigmatic and subtle: they were electronic and experimental, made in collaboration with Brian Eno and produced by Tony Visconti.

Perhaps spurred on by the success of those he had influenced, he returned to a more commercially successful (though still highly individual) approach in the late seventies. Of the major artists of the early 1970s, Bowie remains the most respected and influential – a major myth-maker of what he has called 'this age of grand illusions'.

EARLE BROWN (1926...)

American composer. Schooled in the Schillinger system of composition,

Brown was associated with John Cage and David Tudor on the Music for Magnetic Tape project, centred initially at the pioneer Barron studio, during 1952–55. From 1955 to 1960 he assisted in the production of the influential series of new avant-garde music recordings issued by the TIME series 2000 label.

Apart from *Times Five* (1963) for instrumental sounds and tape, realized at the Paris GRM studio, Brown's interest has mainly centred on notation and performance innovation in the traditional concert arena.

DONALD BUCHLA (c 1936...)

American designer and engineer. A pioneer contemporary of Robert Moog in the development of voltage control devices for music synthesis, Buchla collaborated with the San Francisco composer Morton Subotnick during the early 1960s. The Buchla system differs from the Moog in design philosophy, approximating to a mixer in function, whereas the Moog is closer to a musical instrument. An expandable system of components, it is controlled by touch-sensitive plates rather than a keyboard. Preset manually, these allow the generation of non-scalic control voltages. A special feature is that amplitude varies according to the pressure applied to the plate.

Buchla is chiefly known as producer of the first sequencer module, whereby a pre-set array of control voltages, which may be applied at will to the generation or shaping of a signal output, can be operated in sequence automatically at any desired speed over a wide range, and also to repeat automatically as a loop configuration.

The system has been shrewdly described as responding to the 'sound-action' aesthetic of the US West Coast in contrast to the 'pitch-literal' aesthetic of the New York school.

JOHN CAGE (1912...)

American composer and philosopher. The son of an unsuccessful inventor, Cage studied with Henry Cowell, pioneer of the tone cluster, and with Schoenberg, who described the young Cage as 'not a composer, but an inventor – of genius'. In a richly varied career he taught in Moholy-Nagy's Chicago School of Design (1941–42), has collaborated with the dancer Merce Cunningham since 1942, founded the Project of Music for Magnetic Tape with Morton Feldman, Earle Brown and Christian Woolf (1952–55), became a leading proponent of musical chance and indeterminacy, and an active and resourceful pioneer of mixed media performance art. He is also an expert amateur mycologist.

Cage's lifelong involvement with electronic media began with the lecture *The Future of Music: Credo* (1937), which defines a new musical aesthetic and methodology based on film, radio and disc technology. Around this time he developed the prepared piano, an early forebear of the keyboard synthesizer (*Bacchanale*, 1938) and began working with vari-speeded frequency test discs (*Imaginary Landscape I*, 1939). Subsequent works have incorporated radio, pick-up cartridges, contact microphones and feedback circuitry. *Fontana Mix* (1958), a turbulent and exuberant tape collage, was realized at the RAI Milan studio; a decade later he produced *HPSCHD* for harpsichordists, tapes and other media in collaboration with Lejaren Hiller, incorporating computer-generated permutations of Mozart's Musical Dice Game, K.249d, and other masters.

Probably the first, certainly the most consistently forthright and witty exemplar of McLuhan's 'electronic man', Cage is now recognized as the most influential embodiment, musically speaking, of a new sensibility adapted to a world of instant information.

THADDEUS CAHILL (1867–?)

American inventor of the Telharmonium. Cahill was a businessman by temperament, not a musician, and one of a vast number of inventors in the America and Europe of the late nineteenth century who quickly grasped the mass entertainment potential of Edison's telephone and recording discoveries, but whose projects foundered for lack of sufficiently developed technology.

Two significant principles underlie the Telharmonium: a scientific interest in the synthesis of complex tones, as suggested by Helmholtz and elaborated by numerous nineteenth-century organ-derived keyboards, and a business intuition for the rich rewards to be obtained by being the first to pipe music to private homes. In these senses he can be viewed as a significant precursor of Olsen, whose RCA Synthesizer Mk II bears a similar saurian relationship to today's domestic synthesizer, and of the Muzak industry.

JOHN CALE (*c* 1942…)

Welsh composer, guitarist and viola player. As a member of the enormously influential New York group, The Velvet Underground, from 1966 to 1968, Cale was the first rock musician to have also worked with the experimental avant-garde. Classically trained, he had gone to New York a few years earlier on a scholarship to the Eastman Conservatory, but had discontinued his studies and worked with LaMonte Young, playing electric viola. He had met singer and poet Lou Reed in 1964, and joined him in The Velvet Underground on its inception. The group was used by Andy Warhol in his mixed media show, The Exploding Plastic Inevitable. Their uncompromising music and the urban menace of their words produced a cult following,

but neither of the two albums made while Cale was a member were commerically successful. No other group in rock, however, has had such a great influence without having had a hit record.

Cale made a record in collaboration with Terry Riley, *Church of Anthrax* (1971), and several solo albums. He has also worked as a producer and musician with many other artists, including Nico, singer with the original Velvet Underground.

CORNELIUS CARDEW (1936…)

English composer. Born in Gloucestershire, Cardew studied composition at the Royal Academy of Music in London and electronic music at Cologne in 1957–58. His early pieces were influenced by Boulez and Stockhausen, and from 1958 to 1960 he worked as Stockhausen's assistant. From around 1960,

John Cage became a considerable influence, and Cardew's pieces became more indeterminate and his scores more graphic and verbal. *Treatise* (1963–67) is a 193-page score to which performers are to react freely.

He has been closely involved with improvisation, both with jazz musicians in the performance group AMM (although their performances are jazz in no conventional sense), and with musicians and non-musicians in the Scratch Orchestra, which he co-founded in 1969. His highly indeterminate pieces were later replaced by very simple 'popular' works in the early seventies, intended to reflect a strong socialist political philosophy. Cardew has been a great influence on many young British composers of the avant-garde.

WENDY CARLOS (1939…)

American composer-performer. In

1968 the sounds of the Moog synthesizer succeeded where hundreds of baroque instruments had failed: Walter Carlos's album of electronic arrangements, *Switched On Bach*, made the old master a bestseller, becoming first a gold and then a platinum record. The sequel, *The Well-Tempered Synthesizer*, was also a success, exploiting a market for souped-up baroque and for synthesized music in general.

In 1972 Walter Carlos underwent a sex-change operation and became Wendy. She continued with her electronic transcriptions as before, and composed on the synthesizer as well, creating a suite, *Sonic Seasonings*, and writing music for the film *A Clockwork Orange*. The fame of her recordings has been a mixed blessing both for her and for electronic music in general. Her Moog arrangements have tended to overshadow her efforts as a composer and, while introducing electronic timbres to a wide audience, the records have accustomed the public to think of the synthesizer as a kind of trendy electric piano.

TRISTRAM CARY (1925…)

English composer. After studying science and philosophy at Oxford, Cary embarked on a musical career, having experimented in the application of electronics to music following his Navy experience as a radar technician. During the fifties and early sixties he was one of a select few pioneers of electronic music in Britain. To finance his own research, he composed incidental music for radio, films and television. In 1968 he founded a studio at the Royal College of Music in London, and the following year, in partnership with the brilliant systems designer Peter Zinovieff, founded Electronic Music Studios Ltd, manufacturers of the famous Synthi series. He now teaches at the University of Adelaide in Australia.

The scientist **William Duddell** was one of the leading electrical engineers of his day. He received many honours during his lifetime – and the CBE after his death

D

E

HUGH DAVIES (1943–   )

English composer and instrument-maker. An Oxford graduate, he was assistant to Karlheinz Stockhausen, 1964–66, and a member of the Group Stockhausen ensemble. Since 1967 he has been active in London as a performer, notably with groups The Option Band, Gentle Fire and the Music Improvisation Co., and as director of the electronic music workshop at the University of London, Goldsmiths' College.

Since 1967 he has increasingly specialized in construction and performance of small-scale amplified instruments, fabricated chiefly from audio spare parts and assorted domestic hardware. Davies is best known internationally, however, as compiler of the monumental *International Electronic Music Catalog* (Cambridge, Mass., 1968).

LEE DE FOREST (1873–1961)

American inventor. De Forest is generally accepted as the inventor of the oscillator. He also invented the triode, although patent rights were only granted after considerable litigation. The inventor was even sued for fraud in 1912, when he tried to promote devices for which no application could be found. Although his discovery was to have vital significance in the development of radio, his original triode was intended merely as a 'device for amplifying feeble electric currents', as the patent specification of 1906 stated. It is now suggested that at the time he neither realized the triode's possibilities nor fully understood its operation. None the less, the triode has proved to be one of the most significant discoveries of this century.

The son of a Congregational minister, De Forest studied at Yale University, where he obtained his Ph.D, in 1899. He had always been interested in wireless telegraphy, and in ways of improving it: he experimented with a gas-flame coherer before Fleming invented the diode in 1904. De Forest's addition of a third electrode between the cathode and anode was a logical step. From then on he was a prodigious inventor, and was granted over 300 patents in his lifetime; the last, for an automatic telephone dialling system, being granted when he was eighty-four.

WILLIAM DUBOIS DUDDELL (1872–1917)

English scientist. Duddell invented the very first electric musical instrument: the Singing Arc. It has to be admitted, however, that he merely regarded his invention as a laboratory toy, an off-shoot of his main scientific research in wireless telegraphy.

He was educated privately in England and at Cannes, served an apprenticeship in Colchester and entered the City and Guilds School when he was twenty-one. Several scholarships enabled him to continue his studies, and he soon distinguished himself as a brilliant electro-physicist. At the turn of the century, when street lighting was being improved by the use of electricity, serious problems were being encountered with the noise–an irritating whistle–from arc lamps. Duddell was one of several eminent scientists who were called upon to investigate the problem. He made a thorough analysis of the phenomenon and discovered that alterations in the current caused changes in the pitch of the note produced by the arc. The term 'singing arc' had already been coined by the time Duddell, for lecture purposes, rigged up a keyboard capable of producing the notes of the scale.

He was elected President of the society of Electrical Engineers when he was forty, and became a Fellow of the Royal Society the following year.

BRIAN ENO (1948...)

English composer, performer and record producer. A former student at Winchester Art College, Eno achieved prominence as synthesizer player and operator of tape effects for the group Roxy Music, of which he was a member from 1971 to 1973. His membership of the group was characterized by his use of the synthesizer as a sound source and treatment device rather than as a keyboard instrument, an approach still rare in rock music.

His long-standing interest in, and involvement with, avant-garde music resulted in the album *No Pussyfooting* (1973), using complex tape loops to treat the guitar playing of Robert Fripp, and more interestingly in the formation of the Obscure Records label in 1975. This was a label for avant-garde and experimental music which he was able to start as the result of his rock career. Many of the leading figures of the English avant-garde were involved, either as performers or composers: Cornelius Cardew, Christopher Hobbs, Gavin Bryars, John White, Michael Nyman, Hugh Davies and members of the Scratch Orchestra, the Portsmouth Sinfonia and the Penguin Café Orchestra. The works tended to be quiet and gentle, often aspiring to a kind of superior Muzak, an approach typified by Eno's own *Discreet Music*, in which the 'score' is the diagram of the tape delay system used. Several of Eno's other albums have used the idea of environmental music, notably the *Music for Airports*.

More straightforward activities in the rock field have included several solo albums, collaboration with David Bowie on some of his most electronic records, and work as a producer. He also wrote the music for the homosexual film with Latin dialogue *Sebastiane*, and published *Oblique Strategies*, a series of aphorisms printed on cards, for use in the recording studio.

The unscheduled appearance of **Jimi Hendrix** at the 1969 Woodstock concert was for rock fans the climax to an unforgettable occasion. It was one of his last appearances; he died the following year in London

H

The Hammond organ, and its inventor

LAURENS HAMMOND
(1895–1973)

American inventor. Hammond is principally remembered for the electric organ which bears his name. First put on the market in 1935, it was so superior to other instruments in the same field that it became an immediate success. In December of that year alone, fifty-one churches in the United States installed Hammond organs, and by the end of 1937 about 3000 instruments had been sold.

Although the fortune which he also made enabled him eventually to retire to a château in the Loire Valley, the invention of the organ did not exhaust his creative genius. He was also responsible for the design and invention of devices such as the electric clock, stereoscopic motion pictures and stage effects for the Ziegfeld Follies. More remarkably, his designs for parts of guided missiles contributed towards the ultimate construction of space rockets. During his lifetime he received many honours, including the

Wetherill Medal from the Franklin Institute.

JIMI HENDRIX (1942–70)

American guitarist, composer and singer. Born in Seattle, far from the centres of rock and roll, in four turbulent years Hendrix transformed rock music and the art of rock guitar. In 1966, after he had worked as a backing musician for R & B and soul artists such as Little Richard, B. B. King and Wilson Pickett, Chas. Chandler of The Animals took him to London and around him created The Jimi Hendrix Experience.

Hendrix's effect was massive and immediate. No other guitarist had made the instrument such an intense, personal voice. He utilized electronic resources like feedback and wah-wah pedal to produce an astonishing range of snarls, whines and howls, all delivered at bone-shattering volume. His stage demeanour increased the atmosphere of passion, violence and sensuality. As well as exaggerating the guitar's phallic symbolism, he plucked it with his teeth, stroked it, crooned to it and sometimes, as a climax to his

performance, even smashed it.

His act at the 1967 Monterey Festival was a sensation, ending in a blaze of publicity when he set fire to his guitar. From then on, his appearances created a furore everywhere, reflected in the sales of albums such as *Are You Experienced?* and *Electric Ladyland*. But 'the first black performer to take on white rock and roll head on' became increasingly beset by problems. He was arrested for drug possession. Friction within the band erupted in a fight between him and his bass player, and ended with a night in jail. Strained and unsure of himself, he told one reporter: 'I've got to get out.' In September 1970, Hendrix died from an overdose of barbiturates.

PIERRE HENRY (1927…)

French composer. Henry was the musically trained partner of Pierre Schaeffer, who with him founded the Groupe de Recherches Musicales under the aegis of the French Radio and Television network. He studied composition at the Paris Conservatoire; Messiaen and Nadia Boulanger were among his

teachers. His early pieces were written in collaboration with Schaeffer, but later (in 1958) he established a private electronic music studio.

Among Henry's compositions are *Le Voyage* (1961–63), based on the Tibetan Book of the Dead, and *Messe de Liverpool*, written for the consecration in 1967 of the new Roman Catholic cathedral.

BERNARD HERRMANN
(1911–75)

American composer. Herrmann's music is familiar to the public through his scores for great film classics such as *Citizen Kane* and *Psycho*. Although basically his music is written for orchestra, from early on he used electronic instruments and other devices to enhance the overall tone colour. He used four theremins in *The Day the Earth Stood Still*, as well as a sine wave generator in the title sequence. Many of his innovative techniques were used in his music for the film *The Devil and Daniel Webster*. These included painting the characteristic sound pattern of the overtones of C on to the sound-

track, so producing a phantom fundamental; the superimposition of six tracks of violin notes played in several different ways; and the singing of telegraph wires.

LEJAREN HILLER (1924…)

American composer. Hiller's *Illiac Suite* (1957) for string quartet was the first substantial work written with the aid of a computer. The composer studied

chemistry at Princeton University, and music as a subsidiary subject with Roger Sessions and Milton Babbitt. After graduation he worked as a research chemist for a while, at the same time continuing his activities in music. His later work with computers led to his programming of the *Illiac Suite* in collaboration with Leonard Isaacson. In 1958 he obtained a teaching post in music at the University of Illinois, and became director of the Experimental Music Studio there.

His earlier compositions were written for conventional instruments in a traditional medium, but he later turned to composition with electronic instruments. HPSCHD (1968), for one to seven harpsichords and one to fifty-one tape recorders, written in collaboration with John Cage, is perhaps is best-known work. Since 1964 his pieces have tended to include dramatic and visual elements.

Although **Bernard Herrmann** calls for unusual instruments in his film scores, he claimed 'there are no new sounds, only new ideas'

J

JEAN-MICHEL JARRE
(1948...)

French composer. Jarre is one of the most successful young European composers in the field of commercial electronic music. He has composed for films, advertising jingles and made the best-selling album *Oxygène*. His father was Maurice Jarre, who has written many distinguished film scores, including the Oscar-winning *Doctor Zhivago*.

While still at school, Jean-Michel took private lessons at the Paris Conservatoire, then studied contemporary and electronic music at the Group de Recherches Musicales. Leaving without a degree, he set up his own recording studio to create music that would be both personally satisfying and publicly accessible.

Since 1971 he has written for opera, ballet and films, as well as composing songs for Françoise Hardy, jingles for Pepsi-Cola and background music for airports and department stores. Jarre refuses to categorize his music, seeing every assignment as a new opportunity to expand his personal style.

ANDRÉ JOLIVET (1905–74)

French composer. An individual and original musician, Jolivet would be better known outside France were he not overshadowed by Messiaen. When he met Varèse at a concert in 1928, he became a frequent visitor to the older man's house, and the composer's only pupil.

Jolivet was a strenuous opponent of serialism, believing that music must never be divorced from humanity; but his interest in oriental melody and exotic tunings, as well as a fondness for strange timbres, led him to exploit the unusual qualities of the ondes martenot, for which he wrote a concerto, and a duo, *Poèmes,* for ondes martenot and piano.

L

OTTO LUENING (1900…)

American composer. Luening was born in Milwaukee, but studied music at the State Academy in Munich and the Zürich conservatoire. He had concentrated on flute playing and conducting, but while in Zürich began his long association with avant-garde and electronic music by having composition lessons from Busoni. He returned to America as director of the opera department at the Eastman School of Music in 1925, which he followed with a series of academic appointments.

Luening became very active in the field of electronic composition from 1952 onwards, producing some of the first tape compositions in the USA both on his own and with Ussachevsky. Among his own compositions are *Fantasy in Space* (1952), using flute and tape; *Gargoyles* (1960), for violin and electronic sounds; and *Synthesis* (1962), for electronic sounds and symphony orchestra. Among the works he has produced with Ussachevsky are: *Poem in Cycles and Bells* (1954), and the score for Orson Welles's *King Lear*. He co-founded, with Milton Babbitt, the Columbia-Princeton Electronic Music Center, which quickly became of focal importance. Luening has remained a leading figure in American music. His own style is eclectic and frequently witty.

Jean-Michel Jarre surrounded by an array of electronic keyboards in the Place de la Concorde. His particular blend of talent and experience have made his albums *Oxygène* and *Equinoxe* best-sellers.

M

BRUNO MADERNA (1920–73)

Italian conductor and composer. A leader of the Italian avant-garde, in 1955 Maderna founded an experimental studio in Milan with Luciano Berio. His principal compositions combine electronic music with live performance (not necessarily musical). In his *Hyperion*, for instance, a flautist unpacks four flutes of different sizes, but the sound which is eventually heard is that of a prerecorded and vastly amplified fortissimo.

In 1963, at the Venice Festival of Contemporary Music, Maderna took part in an extraordinary antiphonal battle with the composer Xenakis; the latter had contributed a composition for two orchestras and two conductors, in which the degree of audience acclaim was regarded as one of the work's 'stochaic parameters'. As a conductor, Maderna was highly regarded for his facility in handling the most complex and difficult scores.

JÖRG MAGER (1880–1939)

German inventor and composer. Mager was one of the pioneers in the field of electric musical instrument construction. Unlike Hammond, whose instruments were built to serve the performance of existing music, Mager was interested in building an instrument which could extend the frontiers of musical composition.

He began constructing prototypes before the First World War, with the object of building an instrument that could produce microtonal intervals. Eventually he constructed the Sphaerophon, an instrument in which the vibrations are generated by feedback generators. A demonstration at Donaueschingen in 1926 aroused considerable interest and the following year, at a seminar in Frankfurt, he produced another instrument, the Kaleidophon, on which glissando chords were possible. This was soon followed by two other instruments, the Elektrophon and the Partiturophon.

Mager's skills were put to unexpected use when he was asked by the Bayreuth Opera House in 1931 to create the deep bell sounds called for in the score of Wagner's *Parsifal*, almost impossible to produce in the orchestral pit by conventional means. In 1932 he composed an electronic score for a production of Goethe's *Faust* in Darmstadt, and he followed this in 1936 with *Vision Musik*, incidental music for a film. Mager is widely seen as the father of German electro-musical research.

MAURICE MARTENOT
(1898–1980)

French inventor. Although Martenot's name has been perpetuated in several musical scores which call for the instrument he invented, the instruments themselves are rarely found outside France. But between the wars, the ondes martenot had an international impact on music.

Martenot was born in Paris; he studied piano, cello and composition at the Conservatoire there. His first instruments were produced in 1928; during the following ten years Maurice and his sister Ginette were to give literally hundreds of concert demonstrations, culminating in an appearance at the Exposition Universelle in 1938, when eight of the instruments were played in ensemble with orchestral accompaniment. The instrument's curious timbres, and the keyboard capable of producing microtonal effects, attracted great attention. Composers of film and incidental music were not slow to realize the possibilities of the exotic sounds made by the ondes, while France's leading composers for the concert platform saw it as the instrument of the future, and composed for it accordingly.

Messiaen wrote for it in his *Fête des*

belles eaux, and incorporated it in a larger tapestry of sound in his *Turangalîla* symphony. Several other composers – Milhaud, Honegger and Ibert, for example – used it in smaller works.

Armed with a teaching manual (given the seal of respectability with a preface by Alfred Cortot), Martenot founded a school, somewhat modestly called L'École d'art Martenot, at Neuilly, with branches at most of the regional music schools. He was also in charge of the teaching of the ondes martenot at the Paris Conservatoire.

GEORGE MARTIN (1926...)

English producer and composer. The course of the Beatles' incredible career might have been very different without George Martin. A house producer for EMI, he auditioned them on 6 June 1963, as a result of which he signed them to Parlophone – the label of which he was managing director. Initially he was responsible for capturing their rock and roll energy on record. Then, as their compositions became increasingly ambitious, he was relied on to translate their sometimes vague intuitions into sound.

Martin's musical training and recording skill were often tested by the Beatles' untutored genius. John Lennon, for instance, wanted to combine two separate takes of 'Strawberry Fields Forever', though they were in different tempos and keys. He left the problem with Martin, who solved it by speeding up the tape of the slower, lower version. Many of his own suggestions, such as the use of a random tape collage on *Sergeant Pepper*, were readily accepted.

Martin always paid full tribute to the Beatles' talent and originality. But he believed too that they required some kind of experienced guidance to bring out their best, and the later and individual chapters of their careers may

bear him out. Martin himself, as an independent producer, has had many further successes. After leaving EMI he started the AIR studios, with a successful and influential London complex and an exotic but highly equipped offshoot on a Caribbean island.

OLIVIER MESSIAEN (1908...)

French composer. Indisputably one of the greatest composers of the century, Messiaen has had a tremendous influence – through his music, and as a teacher – on a whole post-war generation of musicians, which includes Stockhausen and Boulez. He came from a literary family: his mother was a poet and his father a translator. He entered the Paris Conservatoire when he was eleven and remained there until he was twenty-one, taking several first prizes.

His interests in music have stretched far beyond the confines of present-day Western European culture: he has

taken into his idiom medieval plainchant, Indian ragas, the gamelan orchestras of Indonesia and bird song. Also inseparable from his music is his profound Catholic faith. Stockhausen has described Messiaen's music as a crucible of material in fusion. Although his best-known works are for acoustic instruments, several of his pieces include the ondes martenot, which appear in his *Turangalîla* symphony, *Fêtes des belles eaux* (for an ensemble of the instruments), *Deux monodies en quart de ton* and *Trois Liturgies de la Présence Divine*, for female chorus, piano, ondes martenot and orchestra.

It was one of his less well-known works, *Mode de valeurs et d'intensités* (1949), which was to have a far-reaching influence on the thinking of composers such as Boulez and Stockhausen. In this piece, Messiaen showed for the first time that serial music need not confine itself to the quantities of pitch alone.

ROBERT MOOG (1934…)

The name of Moog is synonymous with synthesizers. Moog became interested in electronic musical instruments while a student, and made theremins to supplement his income while studying engineering at Cornell University. He first exhibited some electronic modules at the New York Engineering Society convention in 1964. During the mid-1960s his company developed a synthesizer, using voltage control and recently available cheap semiconductors. Although still a complex machine, his synthesizer was of manageable proportions, and capable of reasonable ease of programming by means of patch boards and a piano-type keyboard. The use of Moog equipment by the Beach Boys (on 'Good Vibrations') and the Beatles in 1967, and in Walter Carlos's 'Switched-on Bach' in 1968 was responsible for the rapid public acceptance of the synthesizer.

Moog's creative skills and sound business sense were seminal to the rapid development of more compact, versatile and inexpensive instruments, including polyphonic synthesizers, though this availability of a seductive new instrument to large numbers of rock musicians may be seen as the cause of a whole new alphabet of aural clichés. Moog seems destined to remain inextricably linked with his instrument as Singer with the sewing machine.

GORDON MUMMA (1935…)

American composer. Mumma was one of the first to introduce computer participation into live performance, and coined the term 'cybersonics' to describe the process.

As a boy he learned french horn and piano, and entered the University of Michigan to study theory and composition. In 1958 he became a co-founder with Robert Ashley of the Cooperative Studio for Electronic Music at Ann Arbor, Michigan, which became a centre for mixed-media performance, including the ONCE group. He was also a composer and musician with the Merce Cunningham dance group. His interest in cybernetics and the influence of the dance group contributed to the evolution of his style, which is not limited by the composer's ideas and the performer's interpretations, but expanded by the inclusion of a third variable: that of a computer making further decisions during the performance. He has also worked with jazz musicians, for example with pianist Bob James on *Peasant Boy* (1965).

Among his other works are *Le Corbusier* for orchestra, organ and cybersonic console; and *Conspiracy 8* for bowed cross-cut saw, amplifiers, oscillators, tele-type and cathode-ray tube display, time-sharing digital computer with data link, and seven auxiliary performers.

Mike Oldfield's fame rests principally on his *Tubular Bells*; later recordings have been *Ommadawn* and *Boxed*

N

O

LUIGI NONO (1924...)

Italian composer. Nono studied law at Padua, simultaneously taking a music course in Venice. His first studies in composition were with Malipiero, then later with Maderna. He rose to prominence through Maderna's championing of his music at Darmstadt and Donaueschingen, and quickly became known as a leading figure of the post war avant-garde.

In 1955 he wrote *Incontri*, which was to be a watershed in his musical development. From then on he began to experiment with vocal timbres, and added to the serialization of dynamics and timbres (used by Boulez and others), the serialization of vocal utterances. From 1963 he worked almost exclusively with electronic techniques.

He has given a great deal of his time to political activities, being a prominent member of the Communist Party in Venice, and much of his music is imbued with political idealism. It is debatable whether his use of street cries in *Contrapunto dialettico* or factory noises in *La Fabbrica illuminata* has any relevance in making the music more proletarian. His claims that by turning his back on the progress of European music he is able to approach the worker, farmer and guerilla, presumes that the average factory hand would prefer an evening of avant-garde music to a concert by The Rolling Stones or Petula Clark.

MIKE OLDFIELD (1953...)

English musician and record producer. Oldfield made a series of records during the 1970s which used the multi-tracking facilities of the commercial recording studio as a major means of producing a distinctive musical style and texture. The origins of his techniques in the production of the first of these, *Tubular Bells* (1973), little suggested its phenomenal world-wide success. A young folk-oriented guitarist, Oldfield started work on it as a 'demo', using any studio time he could get. It was finally completed to become Virgin Records' first release. Its use of simple melodic phrases repeated again and again, with suggestions of classical, folk and rock music, gave it a very wide appeal, and world sales of over nine million. It was also used as incidental music for the film *The Exorcist*.

Subsequent records have not equalled its sales but have continued to develop the same ideas, with perhaps an increasing trend towards English folkiness – seen in *Hergest Ridge* (1974). *Tubular Bells* has been orchestrated by the English schoolteacher and composer David Bedford.

Luigi Nono. His electronic music tends to be constructed out of fragmented vocal sounds, which are transformed electronically, and also from similar principles that he applies instrumentally, i.e. *musique concrète*. He married Schoenberg's daughter, Nuria, in 1955

STEVE REICH (1936...)

American composer and performer. Reich has said he is committed to 'music which works exclusively with gradual changes in time'. His compositions are for chamber groups playing very basic rhythmic and melodic patterns seemingly in unison. But Reich's art depends on subtle variations in timing that develop through the course of a performance.

His interest in this kind of musical process comes from his experience of electronic music. Pieces like *It's gonna rain* (1965) and *Come out* (1966) are tape compositions in which a single spoken phrase is repeated by means of tape loops. By carefully manipulating their relative speeds, Reich explores the sounds that make up the phrases. He plays them against each other, producing unexpected nuances of pitch and rhythm. Later works, such as *Four organs* (1970) and *Music for 18 instruments* (1976), apply these complex principles to more conventional instruments.

Reich's music has acquired a surprising following in both popular and classical circles. Audiences have found it spacious, hypnotic and relaxing; but Reich's intention is still 'to facilitate closely detailed listening'.

TERRY RILEY (1935...)

American composer and performer. Working with tape recorders attracted Riley (as it did Reich) to the potential of musical repetition. He first applied the principle in an unconventional piece for conventional instruments. *In C* (1964). Playable by any kind of ensemble, the work provides basic modal figures over an unvarying rhythm which the performers weave into patterns. The recorded version excited rock fans as well as members of the avant-garde, and Riley's subsequent pieces have contrived to maintain this interest.

Works of the late sixties such as *Poppy Nogood and the Phantom Band* and *A Rainbow in Curved Air* utilize electronic instruments and tape. By multi-tracking, Riley himself played all the music, creating a mesmerizing effect by slow, varied repetition. He has also acquired a reputation as a solo performer, playing electric organ or soprano saxophone against this kind of ostinato, bringing forth the same organically expanding structures. Riley's 'musical hall of mirrors' is reflected in his 1971 album, *Persian Surgery Dervishes*.

LUIGI RUSSOLO (1885–1947)

Italian painter, composer and polemicist. Russolo originally trained as a painter, but became active as a prominent figure in the Futurist movement partly through his experiments in music. Although not a composer of electronic music, nevertheless, in breaking through the sound barriers of accepted conventions he was the forerunner of all composers who have used the medium of *musique concrète*.

In 1912 he constructed a series of *intonarumori* or noise machines which operated on similar principles to theatrical thunder machines, football rattles and bird scarers. In appearance they resembled wooden chests with megaphones in front. At the back, or side, were handles which rotated pallets, etc., acting on a membrane. His *psofarmoni* were keyboard 'noise' instruments which in some ways anticipated later musical experiments by John Cage.

S

PIERRE SCHAEFFER
(1910...)

French composer. Schaeffer, a radio
sound engineer, coined the term *musique concrète* to refer to music which
was created from existing sounds in
the studio, as distinct from music that
was composed on paper. The term
came to be used to distinguish music
using natural sounds from pure electronic music. He began to experiment
in 1948; his first work, a rondo-like
assembly of train sounds which he
found in the effects library, used
unmodified – and hence recognizable – sounds. Later works used
sounds which had been played at a
different pitch, or run in reverse, to
create altogether new noises; tape editing also played an important part, as
did the addition of echo and other
effects.

Schaeffer was joined by Pierre
Henry, with whom he collaborated on
his *Symphonie pour un homme seul* and
most of his other compositions. In 1950
they were joined by the sound
engineer Jacques Pollin, who began to
construct equipment specifically for
the purpose of composition. Some of
the works which bear Schaeffer's name
(*Orphée 53, Le Capitaine Némo*) are the
product of corporate efforts.

Schaeffer has always actively cooperated with other composers: many
of the electronic compositions of Varèse and Boulez, as well as Stockhausen, Berio and Xenakis, have been
the product of the Paris studio.

PHIL SPECTOR (1940...)

American producer and composer. At
sixteen, Phil Spector switched his
allegiance from jazz to rock because
rock was 'what people respond to
today'. By the time he was twenty-one,
his ability to predict those responses
had made him a millionaire.

His own group, *The Teddy Bears*, had

a 1958 hit in 'To Know Him is to Love Him', a title Spector supposedly based on his father's epitaph. But he came into his own as a producer, first for Atlantic Records, then for his own company, Philles. Spector controlled every aspect of his output. He selected and trained his stars, and chose and sometimes wrote their material. Above all he dominated their recordings. The Crystals' 'He's a Rebel' was his first huge hit in 1962, but his greatest success came in 1964 with 'You've Lost That Lovin' Feelin'' by the Righteous Brothers. Called 'the ultimate pop record', it featured Spector's 'Wall of Sound', an almost overwhelming complex of echoes and effects created electronically.

One of Spector's few setbacks was his special Christmas album, *A Christmas Gift to You*, which failed because President Kennedy was killed on the day of its release. Another was the 1966 'River Deep, Mountain High' by Ike and Tina Turner, which Spector considered his masterpiece. Blaming its failure on professional jealousy, he abruptly retired. He has produced occasional records since, particularly for the individual Beatles. But basically he has kept to himself, a far cry from the days when he was 'The First Tycoon of Teen'.

KARLHEINZ STOCKHAUSEN (1928...)

German composer. Stockhausen is probably the best-known and most consistently polemical composer of the European avant-garde. Since 1953 most of his work has been at least partly electronic.

His pre-electronic compositions show the influence of Schoenberg, Bartók and Webern. The latter influence, particularly Webern's later works, became more pronounced in 1952-53, when Stockhausen was studying composition with Messiaen

in Paris. It was also at this time that he met Boulez. He espoused the idea of 'total serialism', the application of a series to musical values other than pitch, already used by Messiaen, and it was this compositional principle which he used when in 1953 he started work on the electronic *Studies I & II* at the newly established studio in Cologne.

These works required an enormous amount of painstaking preparation both in building up the timbre of each note from individual sine waves, and in many edits. They were among the first electronic works to have a precisely notated score, and well demonstrate the thoroughness of Stockhausen's approach and his tremendous capacity for work. He later became director of the Cologne studio. Later electronic works used instruments (*Kontakte*, 1959) and voices (*Gesang der Jünglinge*, 1955–56) as well as electronic devices.

His works from the mid-fifties on became less strictly organized, allowing different sections of a piece to be played in varying orders. Although this procedure, known as 'mobile form' (used in *Klavierstück XI* in 1956), allows the performer to determine certain elements of the performance, it is not indeterminate in the Cageian sense, since all the music played is notated. Later works became much freer, the scores establishing the methods of sound production and the relationships between performers.

Stockhausen has written numerous articles (at one time co-editing the influential magazine *Die Reihe*), has had all his music published in large, complicated and often wordy scores, and nearly all of it issued on record (DGG list twenty-nine available works in their 1980 catalogue). He has studied a wide range of scientific and philosophical subjects, many of which have had an influence on his music, in the late 1960s getting heavily into Eastern and mystical topics. He appears to

relish being a superstar of the avant-garde; and his guru-like presence, long haired and white shirted, became familiar to adventurous concertgoers of the 1970s.

MORTON SUBOTNICK (1933...)

American composer. Subotnick has the distinction of being the first composer to be specifically commissioned to write electronic music for a record company (Nonesuch). The first of these works was *Silver Apples of the Moon* (1967), and the second *The Wild Bull* (1968) for synthesizer.

Subotnick studied at Mills College, Oakland, the composer Darius Milhaud being among his teachers there. He later joined the faculty, and was a founder of the Mills Performing Group and the San Francisco Tape Music Center. His music is generally based on electronically generated rather than natural sounds (as used in *musique concrète*), and most of his purely 'sound' works are composed for tape performance, such as *Realities 1–2*, and the works referred to above. Composers who write for tape exclusively soon become aware of a quandary which faces an audience who wish to applaud (or otherwise react to) a work performed by a machine. Because of this, from 1960 Subotnick expanded into theatre, or multi-media, works such as his *Electronic Chamber* for electronically operated lighting effects, sounds and eight players; or his *Concert*, where a woodwind quintet performs extracts from the established repertoire which become changed electronically to the accompaniment of twelve spotlights and two film projectors. His works have also taken on a degree of public participation: in his *Music for Elevators*, installed at 77 Water Street, New York, the push buttons of the elevators activated tape loops of rhythmic and melodic patterns.

Isao Tomita, creator of *Snowflakes are Dancing*. The *Arabesque* is one of the most attractive tracks of these synthesizer versions of Debussy's piano music

LEON THEREMIN
(1896–c 1945)

Russian inventor. Born in St Petersburg, Theremin studied physics at the university there, and also cello at the Musical Institute. In 1919 he was appointed director of the Laboratory of Electrical Oscillations in the Leningrad Physico-Technical Institute, and embarked upon a project which combined his interests in physics and music. The resulting instrument was demonstrated to the All-Union Electrical Congress in 1920. In 1928 the Theremins (inventor and invention) went to the USA; the instrument was patented and put into production the following year. The unusual sweeping sound produced by the theremin, which made no attempt to imitate a conventional instrument, remained in vogue for more than twenty years and was often featured as a novelty act in variety shows.

This was not Theremin's only invention; he also patented a keyboard instrument, and a form of electric cello. The conductor Stokowski used the theremin bass in the Philadelphia Orchestra to give the bass line a stronger support. The most committed use of the theremin is probably in Bernard Herrmann's score for the film *The Day the Earth Stood Still* (1951), which uses two theremins, a theremin violin and a theremin bass.

ISAO TOMITA (1932...)

Japanese electronic composer and performer. In 1974, with the release of the album *Snowflakes are Dancing*, the reputation of a new virtuoso of the synthesizer became assured. The Japanese wizard's electronic versions of pieces by Debussy delighted pop and classical fans by their intriguing and witty sonorities.

Tomita had had wide experience at home before becoming an interna-

tional bestseller. He had written for films and television, amateur choral societies, and even won a commission to provide a theme for the Japanese Olympic team. But his real love was electronic, and in 1973 he founded Plasma Music, a group devoted to all aspects of synthesized music. The unit has toured internationally as well as recorded.

Albums following *Snowflakes are Dancing*, imaginative interpretations of Stravinsky and Mussorgsky, have confirmed Tomita's staying power.

FRIEDRICH TRAUTWEIN
(1888–1956)

German inventor. Born in Würzburg, Trautwein trained as an engineer and later became a lecturer in physics. By 1930 he had developed an instrument for producing sounds electronically. Originally called the Elektrophon (and later the Trautonium to distinguish it from other electrophonic instruments), it attracted the attention of several eminent musicians, such as Hindemith (who wrote a concerto for it) and Richard Strauss.

In 1936 he became professor of musical acoustics at the Berlin Hochschule für Musik, and after the Second World War took an important post at the Schumann Conservatoire in Düsseldorf. He published a number of papers,

among them one on the substance and objectives of electronic music and one on the problems of listening.

The importance of the Trautonium in the development of electronic music lies partly in the works which were written for it, but also in that it was often used as a starting point for the construction of electronic scores (especially in the form of the Mixtur-Trautonium, developed after the war by Trautwein's pupil Oskar Sala).

DAVID TUDOR (1926...)

American pianist and composer. Having studied piano, organ and composition, Tudor became a church organist while still a boy (at St Mark's, Philadelphia). By his early twenties he had begun the association with modern music which was to dominate his life, teaching piano at the Contemporary Music School in New York.

In 1948 he began to work with Cage, with whom he has worked closely ever since. As a musician with the Merce Cunningham Dance Co., as a member of Cage's project of music for magnetic tape and as a performer, composer and teacher, he has long been in the forefront of contemporary music.

The works Tudor has premièred probably constitute the most important body of experimental instrumental music this century, many of them being written specially for him. They include Cage's *Cartridge Music* and *Variations II* and *III*, the first American performances of Stockhausen's *Kontakte* and Boulez's Piano Sonata no. 2.

Tudor's own compositions have used multiple resources, musical and visual, as in *Rainforest* (1968), which parallels an ecological system using 'instrumental loudspeakers' made of different acoustic materials to 'recycle' sounds; and *Video/Laser I* and *II* (1969–70), which use the visual resources implied in the title, the first such use of lasers with music.

U

VLADIMIR USSACHEVSKY (1911...)

American composer. Ussachevsky's name is linked with the Columbia-Princeton Electronic Music Center, which he helped to found with Luening and Babbitt. He was born in Manchuria of Russian parents, and went to the USA in 1930. He took a general course at Pomona College, California, before going on to the Eastman School of Music. In 1947 he took a post teaching music at Princeton University, where he developed an interest in electronic composition and began to produce a number of compositions in the medium. His *Piece for tape recorder* uses sounds of gong, cymbal and piano transformed by being played at altered speeds.

After the establishment of the Electronic Music Center, Ussachevsky collaborated with Luening and others in the score for CBS TV's *An Incredible Voyage*, and with Luening in the *Poem in Cycles and Bells*.

V

EDGARD VARÈSE (1883–1965)

French composer. Varèse, born in the same year as Anton Webern, was virtually a founder member of the avant-garde. Outstandingly original and uncompromising, his ideas and music are as radical today as they were two generations ago. In 1917 he was dreaming of instruments which could offer 'a whole new world of unsuspected sounds'. Even within the limited means of a wind septet and double-bass, as in his botanically titled *Octandre*, he was able to push the boundaries of musical vocabulary to unexpected horizons.

He was given his first lessons in harmony and counterpoint in Turin, when his family – his mother was Italian – moved there, but he returned to Paris in 1903 and studied with d'Indy at the Schola Cantorum. From his mid-twenties he travelled frequently between Berlin and Paris, meeting many notable composers of the day. He became established as a conductor and, being rejected for military service at the outset of the First World War because of ill-health, moved to New York. Not long afterwards he co-founded a society committed to the performance of new works, one of the first of its kind.

Varèse had begun to explore the possibilities of electronic instruments from the late 1920s, and his *Equatorial* uses (in addition to male voice choir, brass, organ and percussion) two theremins. There was a waning of interest in his music until the 1950s, when he was 'discovered' by a new generation of the avant-garde. He began composing with electronic material, and between 1949 and 1954 produced his *Déserts* for instrumental ensemble and tape, having begun the instrumental parts in New York, and finishing the tape at the Paris studio of Pierre Schaeffer. He returned to a conventional medium (soprano, chorus and orchestra) for his unfinished *Nocturnal*, but his last two completed works both involved electronic media.

David Tudor claims that in his *Bandoneon!* (the ! has the mathematical significance of 'factorial') the piece composes itself out of its own elements during performance

111

W

STEVIE WONDER (1950…)

American singer, composer and performer. Born poor, blind and black, Stephen Judkins was a bestselling recording star by the time he was twelve. As Little Stevie Wonder he had his first hit in 1963 and followed it with a series of chart-topping singles like 'Uptight' and 'I Was Made to Love Her'. He owed his success equally to his passionate vocals and his remarkable versatility both as musician and composer.

At twenty-one, having sold 30 million records, the Motown star also came of age musically. He began to concentrate on albums instead of singles and took total control of his recordings, acting as composer, arranger, producer and multi-instrumentalist. His mastery of the synthesizer gave him a subtle range of colours and effects. The resulting albums, like *Inner Visions*, *Music of My Mind* and *Talking Book*, broke free of the Motown sound and gained Stevie Wonder a vast new audience. The music retained all its vitality; but the idiom was personal, astonishingly varied and perfectly realized in the recording.

Songs in the Key of Life appeared in 1976 after three years of preparation, to be followed in 1979 by *The Secret Life of Plants*. Both were hailed as masterpieces, blending energy, sensitivity and assured technique. Audiences may have to wait several years between albums to see what new discoveries the reclusive Stevie Wonder has made. But his work so far shows why the former child prodigy has been described as 'the single most respected performer in the whole of rock music'.

In 1972 **Stevie Wonder** was involved in a road accident which nearly cost him his life. Completely recovering, he produced the award-winning *Fulfillingness' First Finale*

X

IANNIS XENAKIS (1922…)

Romanian-born French composer and architect, of Greek extraction. One of the originators of chance music, Xenakis coined the term 'stochastic' to describe the process. It refers to that theory of probability which states that the greater the number of repetitions of a chance action, the greater the probability of a specified result. Much of his music is derived from mathematical formulae, often calculated with the aid of a computer, transferred to graph paper and thence to musical notation, and finally interpreted by the individual preferences of the composer or performer. The resultant sounds are characterized by dense chord clusters, frequent use of glissandi and elaborately involved individual parts. A corollary of his use of game theory is that performing his music is often like playing in a game, where points are awarded for getting as close as possible to the original score, since much of his music has inbuilt impracticalities making literal live performance of it impossible. For example, in the piano solo *Eryali*, chords are spread out over the whole keyboard. Either notes have to be missed out or some other means of reducing the chords to a playable medium has to be found, such as transposing parts of it up or down a few octaves. This, of course, gives a whole new dimension to interpretation, since exactness and accuracy are out of the question.

Xenakis began his musical studies at the age of twelve, but did a course in engineering at Athens Polytechnic School. During the war he was an active member of the anti-Nazi resistance movement, and was actually under sentence of death when he managed to escape from Greece. He settled in Paris, where he studied music with Honegger, Milhaud and Messiaen, but earned his living as an assistant to the architect Le Corbusier. He became established as an architect himself, and in fact designed one of the pavilions at the 1958 Brussels World Trade Fair. He took French citizenship in 1965, and founded a school of music and related mathematical studies the following year, opening a branch at Illinois University in 1967. His methods and music have had a considerable cross-fertilizing influence on the works of many contemporary composers, including Penderecki.

Y

LaMONTE YOUNG (1935...)

American composer. Young was the originator of a concept which has been termed 'sound environment' to distinguish it from music. Many of his pieces take the form of a background of sustained sound to forms of creative activity or passive meditation on the part of the listener, often using tapes and electronically generated sounds. Many of his compositions have also used lightshows created by his wife, Marian Zazeela. His earlier works, influenced by the sound of wind blowing through the cracks in the log cabin where he was brought up, or the humming of a transformer or aquarium water-pump, often consisted of single chords sustained for a very long time. Later, non-musical elements were introduced into his works (some of which, by accepted definitions, had no music at all); among these are his *Compositions 1961*, nos. 1–29, each of which consists of the same instruction: draw a straight line and follow it.

The titles of his works are often longer than the scores themselves: *The Tortoise, his dreams and journeys* for voice, strings and electronic equipment has two sections whose titles total more than eighty words. In some cases the titles actually constitute the score itself *(Some of them were very old grasshoppers)*. LaMonte Young has also used electronically generated sine waves extrapolated from a section of *The Tortoise* as a sound environment in his home and studio.

Z

FRANK ZAPPA (1940...)

American composer, guitarist and singer. Zappa had played in bars and composed for cheap movies before founding his revolutionary group, The Mothers of Invention, in 1964. The group was the ideal instrument for his large and outrageous talent. Its live performances were as much Theatre of the Absurd as rock. Zappa challenged his audience with Dada events such as his piece 'Dead Air', in which nothing happened until rising irritation out front supplied a climax. He used farfetched comedy, light shows and demonic volume to create irresistible involvement.

But Zappa's musical gifts were indisputable. His songs mocked social inanities and pop music itself. His own taste for surreal comedy appeared in numbers like 'Help, I'm a Rock'. The series of albums that began with *Freak Out* (1966) featured increasingly bold experiments in electronics. He used tape montage to string together wildly contrasting kinds of material – rock, classical music, speaking voices. In *Lumpy Gravy* and *Uncle Meat*, the technique creates startling but coherent compositions.

Zappa disbanded the Mothers in 1969, complaining of ignorant audiences. But he continued to make records, and a 1971 tour was a great success (though it ended in an assault on Zappa by the boyfriend of a female fan). If his releases in the seventies have been less adventurous, they are still clever and accomplished: further attempts, as Zappa himself says, to 'make a special art in an environment hostile to dreams'.

Frank Zappa admits his debt to Varèse and other 'serious' composers. 'Even if you don't like our music', he asserted, 'you have to listen to it because it is everywhere'

113

GLOSSARY

A & R. Stands for 'Artists and Repertoire'. The A & R man in a record company is the talent spotter, on the look-out for artists of promise, and for new material for the musicians already on his books.

ACOUSTIC. A term now used to describe instruments without electrical amplification, e.g. the classical guitar. Acoustics is the science of sound, though the term has also now become associated with the sound qualities – deadness, echo, etc. – of a studio or concert hall.

AMPLIFIER. A device, formerly a vacuum tube or valve *(q.v.)* but now usually a transistor *(q.v.)* for magnifying weak electronic signals sufficiently for them to have a mechanical effect, as in a loudspeaker.

AMPLITUDE. The strength of a signal, resulting in the loudness of a sound.

ANALOGUE. Not divided into numerical steps, but continuous. For example, the fraction 1/3 cannot be shown exactly on a digital calculator, though it can be accurately represented on a slide rule, which is analogue.

CHANNEL. The path whereby a signal is transmitted electronically from one point to another.

CIRCUIT. The complete path of an electric current: for example, the whole assemblage of a batch of electronic equipment.

CLASSIC STUDIO. A studio for the composition of 'serious' taped music, as distinct from the commercial recording studio.

COMPUTER. A highly efficient form of calculating machine, capable of translating verbal, visual and other information into a series of electronic impulses which can be sorted, stored and otherwise manipulated.

CONDENSER. A device for accumulating or increasing the potential of an electric charge.

CROSS FADE. The process of increasing the signal from one channel while decreasing another, to effect a gradual transition from one sound to another.

DADA. An early twentieth-century art movement, deliberately aimed at shocking or scandalizing.

DEMO. Literally 'demonstration'. This is a tape or disc recording made (usually at the artist's own expense) to demonstrate the particular qualities of a group, artist or song.

DIGITAL. Sonically, this refers to information stored in 'bits' and not as a continuous wave. The analogy is with a newspaper photograph, which is made up of thousands of tiny dots.

DIRECT INJECTION. Feeding an electronic instrument directly into a recording desk without the use of microphones.

DOPPLER EFFECT. The change in apparent pitch of a sound, caused by the sound source advancing (and rising in pitch) or retreating (falling in pitch). The effect is caused by the speed of the sound source's actual movement being added to (or subtracted from) the speed of sound. A common example is the drop in pitch of the whistle as a speeding train rushes past an observer.

ECHO. Produced naturally by the reflection of sound off a non-absorbent surface, echo can be obtained electronically in three ways: through a tape recorder, by use of an echo chamber or in a digital delay device.

ELECTROMAGNET. A temporary magnet which can increase or reduce its magnetism instantly in proportion to the electric current supplying it. Familiar uses of electromagnets include setting the core of a loudspeaker in motion, or exciting the magnetic coating on recording tape.

EQ. Literally 'equalization'. This refers to increasing or decreasing certain frequencies in the sound range electronically, in order to achieve a particular sound.

ENVELOPE. A term used for the overall shape of a sound that changes its qualities in time. The attack and decay of a sound or note constitute its envelope. In a device such as a synthesizer, it can be altered by means of an envelope shaper.

FADE. The process of decreasing the signal, whether from an acoustic or electronic sound source.

FEEDBACK. if a loudspeaker is placed within range of a microphone, the latter picks up sound from the speaker, which results in a howl. Such an occurrence used to be accidental, though it is now sometimes pursued by guitarists, etc., specifically for effect.

FILTER. A means of cutting out selected electronic frequencies, and consequently any unwanted qualities, from the sound.

FREQUENCY. The number of events in a given time: for example, the number of vibrations per second.

FUNDAMENTAL. The lowest frequency in a sound (usually of the greatest amplitude), as opposed to its overtones (harmonics).

FUTURISM. An Italian art movement of the early twentieth century, that often exalted the glories of the machine age. Two of its leading exponents were Filippo Marinetti and Luigi Russolo.

FUZZ. An electronc device that makes the sound deliberately harsh and buzzy.

GLISSANDO. Sliding from one note to another, an idiom available only on certain musical instruments, such as the theremin, swanee whistle, musical saw, trombone, etc. and, of course, the voice.

HARMONIC. A sound whose frequency is mathematically related to the fundamental (note sounded). The simplest harmonic is one octave above the fundamental, in the ratio 2:1. (See also p. 35.) They are also called partials or overtones.

HI-FI. High fidelity. High-quality sound reproduction that came into use as a term after the introduction of the long-playing record.

IMPEDANCE. The apparent resistance to an alternating current, comparable with the actual resistance in a direct current. For any given voltage, the impedance determines the amplitude of the alternating current.

INDETERMINACY. A form of composition in which the composer tries to ensure that the resulting sounds are randomly produced. The composer, therefore, is responsible primarily for the situation in which the sounds occur.

INTERRUPTER. A means of interrupting an electric circuit, i.e. a switch.

LOUDSPEAKER. A device for retranslating electric impulses into sound.

MICROPHONE. A device for translating sound waves into electrical impulses.

MICROTONE. A musical interval smaller than a semitone, i.e. the difference between two notes which are closer to each other than any two adjacent notes on the piano keyboard. It follows that it is not possible to play microtones on instruments of fixed pitch, such as the flute or the piano.

MIXER. A device that blends and balances electric signals. Multiple inputs are reduced to a mono or stereo output.

MODULE. Any unit of electronic equipment designed to perform a specific function or functions.

MONITOR. A small loudspeaker or set of headphones that enables the engineer or producer to listen in while a recording is being made.

MULTI-MEDIA. An event or entertainment that combines various media such as sound, light and dance. Strictly speaking, shows like *Oklahoma!* are multi-media, but the term is reserved for presentations that would otherwise defy classification.

MUSIQUE CONCRÈTE. The use of recorded extra-musical sounds (often with various distorting effects) to create electronic music.

OSCILLATOR. A device for producing fluctuations in an electric current.

OVERDUB. To superimpose one recording on top of another.

OVERTONE. One of the harmonics *(q.v.)* above the fundamental note.

PA. Public address system; used to refer to the complete range of microphones, amplifiers and loudspeakers in performance.

PATCHBOARD. An array of jack sockets, etc., which helps to minimize the number of leads needed between instruments or modules.

PHASING. An electronic effect, designed to give the music a particular sound, which deploys two signals in a slightly out of time alignment.

PICK-UP. An electromagnet designed to 'pick up' acoustic vibrations and convert them into electrical impulses, as in an electric guitar or the cartridge of a record player.

POTENTIOMETER. A variable control, usually operated by a rotating knob or slider, as distinct from an on-off interrupter.

PSYCHEDELIC. Literally 'mind turning'. The term was used in the 1960s to describe a wide spectrum of novelties, from hallucinogenic drugs to rock and roll. Kinetic elements are often involved.

REMIX. A reblending, at a later stage in the recording process, of several previously recorded tracks.

REVERB. Reverberation. A form of continuing echo, produced either electronically or acoustically, which gives sound a livelier presence.

RING MODULATOR. A device which combines two frequencies producing either their sum or their difference. Since the result is not in a simple ratio to the other two *(see* **Harmonics***)* the sound produced is harsh or bell-like.

SEQUENCER. A means of storing a sequence of sounds electronically to produce repeated patterns or other effects, such as ostinatos.

SERIAL. A term applied to music which has been composed according to a numerical formula (the series). Originally the series applied only to the pitch of the notes (Schoenberg), but it was later extended to cover the duration and dynamics (Boulez) and even the timbre.

SESSION. A rehearsal, recording or performance: hence 'session player', a freelance musician hired for use in a recording.

SINE WAVE GENERATOR. A device for producing a smooth oscillation, resulting in a sound that contains only one frequency and has no harmonics.

SQUARE WAVE GENERATOR. A device similar in principle to the sine wave generator, but resulting in a more nasal sound.

STOCHASTIC. A form of composition, evolved by Xenakis, in which the overall effect is specified but, within certain limits, details are left to the performer(s).

SYNTHESIZER. An electronic instrument for creating a wide range of musical sounds programmed by the operator, often contained in a single unit.

TAM-TAM. A sonorous oriental gong. Its acoustic peculiarity is that it adapts its apparent pitch to any prevailing pitch in the sound it is accompanying. A complex array of harmonics has led to its frequent use in electronic composition.

TAPE LOOP. An actual loop of recorded tape which, played through a recorder, produces a repeated sound pattern.

TIMBRE. The distinguishing sound qualities (other than pitch or loudness) of a musical sound.

TRANSISTOR. A device which uses the semiconducting properties of certain elements (such as germanium) to amplify weak electric signals, replacing the relatively unwieldy and energy-consuming valve.

TREMOLO. A regular pulsation in loudness. It can be produced electronically or mechanically (usually by a rotating vane).

TWELVE-TONE. A form of serial *(q.v.)* composition in which equal importance is given to each of the notes of the chromatic scale, removing the music from any associations with tonality.

VALVE. A glass or metal case, from which the air has been withdrawn (with the possible substitution of some gas at low pressure) and which is fitted with wire terminals. Electric current passes from one terminal to another in the form of electrons.

VIBRATO. A controlled, slight variation in the pitch of a note. Violinists and guitarists can produce the effect by wobbling the finger on the string.

VOLTAGE CONTROL. A means of adjusting an electrical signal and, as a consequence, the resulting sound.

WAVELENGTH. The measurement of the displacement of molecules in the air (as of sound waves) or electrical field (electromagnetic waves).

WHITE NOISE. Noise which, in theory at least, contains all frequencies at the same intensity. The sonic equivalent of white light.

WHITE NOISE GENERATOR. A device for producing white noise electronically, often used as a sound source through certain filters, resulting in a noise of a certain band-width. The effect is of a pitched hiss.

INDEX
Compiled by Audrey Twine

Page numbers in bold type (**12**) indicate biographical sections and important references. *Italic* page numbers (*12*) direct the reader to illustrations or their captions.

ACKNOWLEDGEMENTS

GENERAL ACKNOWLEDGEMENTS
The author and publishers would like to express their thanks to Hugh Davies and Robin Maconie for their advice and for the generous loan of much invaluable material. They are extremely grateful to Phil Manzanera for making available The Gallery Studio, which appears in many photographs. Special thanks are also due to Jane Mackay, Maggie Colbeck, Jonathan Gill-Skelton, Pete Revill, Geoffrey Smith and Derek Walters.

ARTISTS CREDITS
Jeremy Banks (Studio Briggs Ltd) 25, 38, 39
Hugh Dixon (Spectron Artists) 40, 41
Mark Wilkinson (David Lewis Artists) 95, 100, 101, 104, 105, 106, 107, 110
Les Lawrence – Mezzotints
Commissioned photography by **Peter Loughran,** Jacket and prelims and pages 26, 27, 28, 29, 30, 31, 33, 37, 43 top

PICTURE CREDITS
A: above; C: centre; B: below; L: left; R: right.

3–8: Peter Loughran; 10–11: Smithsonian Institution; 11(A): Knud Peter Petersen, Berlin; 12: Smithsonian Institution; 13 (AL): Knud Peter Petersen, Berlin; 13(AR,CR): BBC Hulton Picture Library; 14(BL): Courtesy of Akademie der Künste; 14–15: Mario Russolo, Cerro di Laveno/Verlag Ullstein; 16(L): Smithsonian Institution; 16(R): Popperfoto;17(A): Smithsonian Institution; 17(BL): Val Wilmer; 17(BR): Knud Peter Petersen, Berlin; 18: Courtesy of National Film Archive/Stills Library; 19(AL): Peter Lertes, Elektrische Musik, Leipzig; 19(AR,BR): Knud Peter Petersen, Berlin; 20(AR): BBC Copyright; 20(BR): Knud Peter Petersen, Berlin; 21(A,C,B): Knud Peter Petersen, Berlin; 22(CL): BBC Hulton Picture Library; 22(CR): BBC Copyright; 22(B): Smithsonian Institution; 24: Mary Evans Picture Library; 25(BR): Paul Brierley; 26–37: Peter Loughran; 39(AL,AR): Popperfoto; 40(BL): Popperfoto; 42–43: BBC Copyright; 43(A): Peter Loughran; 44(A): EMS; 44–45: Peter Loughran; 46(A): © ERA; 46–47: © ERA; 48: © ERA; 50(AL): Courtesy of Akademie der Künste; 50(BL): Allied Artists; 50–51: Universal Edition (London) Limited; 53(A): Courtesy Cunningham Dance Foundation; 53(B): Rex Features; 56–57: Michael Straus; 58: Adrian Boot/London Features International; 61(L,R): Fairlight; 62: Paul Brierley; 65(A): Popperfoto; 65(BL): Erich Auerbach; 65(BC): United Music Publishers Limited; 66: Tate Gallery; 67: Lifritzki-Viollet; 68(BR): Philips-Werke Eindhoven/Verlag Ullstein; 69: Philips-Werke Eindhoven/Verlag Ullstein; 70–71(A): Vautier-de Nanxe; 70–71(B): Mansell Collection; 71(AR): Allied Artists; 73(BR): Fritz Peyer/Polydor; 74: Deutsche Grammophon; 75: Vautier-de Nanxe; 79: David McEnery/Rex Features; 80: Universal Edition (Alfred A Kalmus) Limited; 81(B): Photo: Hervé Gloaguen, courtesy Cunningham Dance Foundation; 84(A): Rex Features; 84(B): Deutsche Grammophon; 85: Kobal Collection; 86(AR): Don Smith/Radio Times; 86–87: Kobal Collection; 88: Photo: Adrian Boot, courtesy of Totton Publicity; 89: Popperfoto; 90(BL): Rex Features; 90–91: London Features International; 92(A): Michael Putland/London Features International; 92–93: Rex Features; 93: London Features International; 94(C): Clive Barda; 94–95: IRCAM/Centre Georges Pompidou; 97(A): London Features International; 97(B): Roberto Massoti/Peters Edition Limited; 98: CBS Records; 99: Eileen Tweedy/Royal Society; 101: Popperfoto; 102–103: Rex Features; 106: Erich Auerbach; 108(A): Rex Features; 108(B): Keystone Press Agency; 111: Courtesy Cunningham Dance Foundation; 112(A): Boosey and Hawkes; 112(B): SKR Photos/London Features International; 113: London Features International.